THE
8 CALENDARS
OF THE
MAYA

"As a traditional Mayan teacher and daykeeper, Hunbatz Men sheds light on the great mystery of Maya/Cherokee oral tradition—the sacred relationship between Earth and the Pleiades. In our sacred tradition, our lives synchronize with the whole cosmos because our Sun is part of the Pleiadian star system. When our hearts are open to our cosmic home, we resonate with the sky's heart, Alcyone, the central star of the Pleiades. This is what I was taught by my Cherokee grandfather Hand, and now Hunbatz Men elucidates the Tzek'eb, the calendars of the Pleaidian Suns. This is a must read for anyone who wonders why humans on Earth feel they are in touch with the Pleiadians."

BARBARA HAND CLOW, AUTHOR OF
*THE MAYAN CODE: TIME ACCELERATION
AND THE AWAKENING OF THE WORLD MIND*
AND *THE PLEIADIAN AGENDA: A NEW
COSMOLOGY FOR THE AGE OF LIGHT*

THE
8 CALENDARS
OF THE
MAYA

The Pleiadian Cycle and the Key to Destiny

HUNBATZ MEN

Translated by Ariel Godwin

Bear & Company
Rochester, Vermont • Toronto, Canada

Bear & Company
One Park Street
Rochester, Vermont 05767
www.BearandCompanyBooks.com

Bear & Company is a division of Inner Traditions International

Originally published in Spanish under the title *Los calendarios astronómicos mayas y Hunab K'u* by Ediciones Horizonte
First U.S. updated and expanded edition published in 2010 by Bear & Company

Library of Congress Cataloging-in-Publication Data

Hunbatz Men, 1941–
  [Calendarios astronómicos mayas y Hunab K'u. English]
  The 8 calendars of the Maya : the pleiadian cycle and the key to destiny / Hunbatz Men ; translated by Ariel Godwin.
      p. cm.
  Includes bibliographical references and index.
  Summary: "Mayan daykeeper Hunbatz Men reveals the multi-calendar system of the Maya that guided the lives of his ancestors and how it can guide us today"—Provided by publisher.
  ISBN 978-1-59143-105-3 (pbk.)
  1. Maya calendar. 2. Maya chronology. 3. Maya cosmology. I. Title. II. Title: Eight calendars of the Maya.
  F1435.3.C14H8613 2010
  529'.32978427—dc22

                                                                    2009036962

Printed and bound in the United States by Versa Press, Inc.

10 9 8 7 6 5 4 3 2 1

Text design by Priscilla Baker
Text layout by Virginia Scott Bowman

This book was typeset in Garamond Premier Pro and Gill Sans with Perpetua, Futura, and Gill Sans used as display typefaces

CONTENTS

This is the memory of the things that happened and they did. Now all is passed. They speak with their own words and thus not all is understood of its meaning; but rightly as it all happened, so it is written. Now again, it all will be very well explained. And perhaps it will not be bad. . . . Truly many were their "real Men." Not in order to sell betrayals did they like to be united some with others; but all that is herein contained or how much needs to be explained is not yet apparent. Those who know it come from our great lineage, that of the Mayan men. These will understand the meaning of what is in here when they read it. And then they will see it and then explain it, and then the obscure signs of the Katún will be clear. It is so because they are the sacerdotes. The sacerdotes ended, but not their name, ancient as they are.

CHILAM BALAM OF CHUMAYEL,
FROM THE SPANISH TRANSLATION
BY ANTONIO MEDIZ BOLIO

FOREWORD

The great value of this work resides in its well-documented content and the author's authenticity as a modern Mayan *hau'k'in,* a traditional Mayan teacher, whose wisdom emerges from his own experience. Hunbatz Men is a true Mayan shaman and daykeeper—an authority on the history, chronology, calendars, and cosmic knowledge of the Mayan civilization. He was born in Wenkal, on the Yucatán Peninsula, in Mexico, and became a disciple of the greatest contemporary champion of Mayan values, Maestro Domingo Martínez Paredes (1899–1983), a professor of the Mayan language at the Universidad Nacional Autónoma de México (National Autonomous University of Mexico) and the author of many works that have brought to light the transcendent nature of the cultural values of this great indigenous civilization.

The study of the Mayan astronomical calendars of pre-Columbian America shows that in the traditional Mayan culture the computation of time was not determined by simple commercial or civil requirements. There was a much loftier goal: to synchronize the lives of human beings and societies to the great cosmic pulsation, to the rhythm of the seasons, and to the other cycles that dictate changes on Earth. Thus by following this rhythm of the universe (the beats of the sky's heart, as the Mayan Popol Vuh describes it), whether through lunar, solar, planetary, stellar, or galactic biorhythms, human beings could avoid all manner of decadence. They could keep themselves in harmony with the universal constant and expand their individual beings far beyond those paltry syllogistic reasonings that fail to achieve a profound observation of certain simple but vital facts.

This cosmic measuring, and its corresponding human synchronization, required an identification of the individual, society, nature, and cosmos—a true and complete *yok' hah Maya* (Mayan yoga). It was a synthetic science, schematized in that invaluable indigenous archeometer: the Mayan astronomical calendars. Here was the key for curing all illnesses and for regenerating the human species, living according to the rules of life, those golden rules that humans did not invent, but rather discovered.

This work by Hunbatz Men complements certain other works published on the same topic, while at the same time enriching them by filling a disconcerting void in the study of the calendars. For this reason, I am pleased to welcome and encourage Hunbatz Men as he continues in the noble task he has set for himself: recovering the legacy of the values of our indigenous races. Indigenous America—our silenced culture—celebrates the publication of this valuable fruit of the Mayan astronomical calendars. Congratulations to Hunbatz Men for such a worthy endeavor, and salutations to all those who preserve faith in our peoples and in the future of our beloved American continent.

IN LAK'ECH,
SAT ARHAT DOMINGO DIAS PORTA

The Venerable Sat Arhat Domingo Dias Porta is a Mayan elder, born and educated in Venezuela. In the 1980s he founded the Movement for the American Indian Solar Cultures.

INTRODUCTION

Our Mayan ancestors were true sages, not simple speculators. They developed an elaborate set of principles that they applied to their religion, their philosophy, their sciences, their architecture, their medicine—indeed, all aspects of their culture.

These principles of the ancient Maya arose out of a single spiritual conception: that the entirety of the cosmos is permeated by sacred energy, and as the cosmos unfolds in countless permutations it constantly reveals the sacred—and thus determines everyday life. In the Mayan way of thinking, human beings are harmonized with divine energy, such that the divine manifests in the myriad forms and beings of the physical world, the world of nature, while the physical world and all its manifestations in nature are reflections of the divine. Being master astronomers, the Mayan sages naturally extended this conception throughout space, such that the whole universe—just like the individual human being—was perceived as a manifestation of divine energy, constantly moving and changing.

Such knowledge was acquired by the ancient Maya through their meticulous observation of nature, which they regarded as their mother and guide. She was the goddess Ixmucane—Mother Earth—one of the thirteen Mayan gods who created the *hombres de maiz,* people of corn, or human beings. She ground yellow, white, red, and black corn and prepared nine different drinks with this mixture. Strength and endurance came from this nourishment, creating the muscles and vigor of the human being, according to the Popol Vuh. Thus Mother Earth's function as a creative force was recognized in the unfolding of the essential processes of life.

Being an expression of the divine, nature (just like the human being) is subject to certain sacred laws, said the Maya of old. They developed an advanced mathematics in which numbers did not specifically relate to quantity, as is often assumed by the modern-day, materially obsessed world; all numbers were expressions of the different frequencies and tones of the divine. So, for example, in the Mayan language the Moon was called *U, Uc,* or *Uh;* it possessed the numerical value of 7. This number ruled women as well as the cycles of generation and conception, since according to the Mayan calendar it was possible to know when one might conceive a son or a daughter. Likewise, by following the lunar cycles, a woman would know the days on which she would not conceive, thereby regulating population in times when food and resources were scarce. This number also represented, among other things as we will see later, the seven powers, or "brains," of the human being.

The Mayan astronomical masters, through the use of mathematics, systematized time in terms of a series of cycles ranging from the macrocosm to the microcosm, and they regarded all such cycles themselves as divine. Hence their renowned calendars became the standard of existence. As expressions of the cosmobiological laws of nature, they ruled all measurements. Thus, for the Maya, their calendars held supreme value: the very existence of human beings was reflected in the calendars, which dictated how they should act to live as part of a harmonious whole. For them it was like having Mother Nature, who had created and formed them and had supported their existence, before them in an expression of impeccable mathematical precision. Through their astronomical calendars, the human being was seen to be the microcosm, part of its great father, the macrocosm—meaning that the great whole is present in each of us. And so the cosmos worked by means of this intelligent energy, this universal energy from which all human beings are created.

One example of the highly evolved astronomical science developed by the Maya is their discovery of the transcendent relationship between the Sun and human beings, which was confirmed by their discovery of the phenomenon of sunspots. For this reason, the Maya called themselves the Children of the Sun. As a result of their observation of 23-year sunspot cycles, the Maya were able to further correlate the relationship between humans and the Sun. The astronomers, who were also astrologers, developed a calendar wheel with 23 years, or "teeth"— information that can be read firsthand in the Porrúa Codex. This is one proof of the great importance that was attributed to this particular sunspot calendar, in which nature becomes cosmobiologically modified by this solar phenomenon—a fact that has been verified by modern-day science. Understanding the phenomenon of sunspots and recognizing its importance, the Maya included it in their book of cosmic calendars as a means of orienting human beings and aiding them in comprehending the past, present, and future—thus helping them to understand and recognize the importance of living in harmony on this beautiful Mother Earth.

We should mention just a few of the many names the Maya gave to the divisions of the temporal cycles: *k'in,* day; *winal,* month; *haab,* year; *uc,* lunar month; *tunben k'ak',* 52 intervals, or years; *k'altun,* 260 intervals, or years; *tzek'eb,* the great year, or 26,000-year cycle.

The Maya used a very special calendar known as the Tzolk'in, a sacred calendar that measures intervals of 260 days, the period of human gestation. This calendar was used for many things, particularly for the synchronization of all the other Mayan calendars. The Tzolk'in was also used in divination, rituals, and possibly for other purposes that have since been forgotten. It was built around the numbers 13 and 20; when these numbers are multiplied, they produce the number 260.

They also used the *xoc kin,* the divinatory days at the beginning of the Mayan year. In this case, the count began on December 22, winter solstice, and lasted for 19 days. During this time the Maya observed the meteorological phenomena that occurred day by day. From these observations they were able to predict whether the year would be favorable or unfavorable. For example, they could predict rainy seasons and droughts, since the climatological situations during this period infallibly determined the way nature would behave throughout the remainder of the year. This has been observed through the course of time.

Pyramids are true producers and transformers of energy, and contemporary science has verified their tremendous power as instruments of positive and negative force. Fully aware of these qualities of pyramids, the Maya adapted them to their calendars, using the pyramidal form as the geometric basis of their chronologies, and using light and darkness to mark the days, weeks, months, years, centuries, and millennia, as can be seen firsthand in the pyramidal temple of Kukulcán, in Chichén Itzá, Mexico, which will be discussed in a later chapter.

Thus the preceding palpably demonstrates the Mayan frame of mind: self-guidance through nature, modified by the movements of the Sun, and consequently by the positions of the Sun, which in turn mark the "minutes" and "hours" on the cosmic clock—times and distances that, rather than simply measuring linear time and material reality, invariably reflect the psychical and physical whole via the cosmobiological rhythms that normalize, or alter, the environment.

And so the Mayan priest of antiquity, who was both an astronomer and an astrologer, would advise each newly married couple to perform the sexual act in accordance with the positions of certain heavenly bodies—principally the Moon, Venus, Jupiter, Mars, Mercury, and Sirius—so that they might choose the sex of their child, as well as its future vocation. In these modern times, all this knowledge has been forgotten. Nowadays when a baby is born, the parents simply watch it grow up, completely unaware of the child's true calling. Herein lies one example of the practical benefits of the Mayan calendars, these chronologies that for our ancestors were true records of the rhythms and biorhythms to which we human beings are subject. For when this knowledge is applied, there is no mystery about the newly engendered being. For this reason, Mayan culture, especially in the form of the Mayan calendars, has astonished scientists and experts today. The Mayan calendars stand in stark contrast to the European calendars, the Gregorian and the Julian, which can only used for telling us what day it is and for determining what tasks we must complete, with no heed paid to our relationship to natural laws, let alone cosmic laws.

Through their precise, accurate, scientific observations, the Maya were able to formulate their astronomical calendars and apply their knowledge of these laws and norms to arrive at a profound understanding of cosmobiological existence, of which we human beings are a part. The greatest testimony to their understanding of these laws of the cosmos is the development of their many calendars, which arose out of their philosophy of *Panche Be:* the search for the root of the truth.

We believe that the Mayan astronomical calendars are capable of teaching us the path that humanity must follow in order to be able to transcend the ignorance into which modern culture, with all its false values and obsession with physical reality, has plunged us. We should therefore examine the Mayan philosophy and try to live according to the principle of *Panche Be*—and then seal our commitment to this path with the Mayan words *In Lak'ech*—"You are I and I am you," a phrase of cosmic fraternity, love, and human brotherhood, speaking to all the manifestations of life.

1

Mayan Roots in Antiquity

In a mysterious, distant, almost-forgotten epoch, people emerged from the great civilizations known as Lemuria and Atlantis, and made their way to other continents—the Americas, Europe, Asia, Africa, Oceania . . .

Science has long sought the lost link between human beings and that earlier animal that, due to phenomenal circumstances, changed its evolutionary path, distancing itself more and more from the ancient biological lineage that gave birth to it in a now-extinct era. Here one may well ask: Where did this prehistoric phenomenon, the human being, first emerge? Was it in Africa? Asia? On some Pacific island? Or was it possibly in the Americas? Or did the first humans appear on a continent that has since been lost to the sea, and to time? A few scholars have even posited that human beings may be of extraterrestrial origin, having come from some other planet in the cosmos to settle on Earth. Let us examine some of the evidence for the roots of the Mayan civilization.

Evidence for Prehistoric Humans in the Americas

Most conventional scholars claim that human beings first emerged in either Africa, Asia, or Europe. However, early human remains found in the late nineteenth century in southernmost South America were discovered by the great Argentinean paleontologists and archaeologists Florentino (1854–1911) and Carlos (1865–1936) Ameghino, two brothers who persistently claimed that they had discovered what they identified as *Homunculus, Tetraprothomo, Triprothomo,* and *Diprothomo.* The brothers' conclusion that humans originated in present-day Argentina during the Tertiary Period (65 million to 1.6 million years ago) have since inspired various hypotheses regarding the ancestry of the peoples of the Americas. These hypotheses have been refuted a priori by some Eurocentric scholars who cling to the assumption that the ancestors of humans never lived in the Americas, and that it is consequently futile to try to find evidence of the first human beings on these American continents.

Nevertheless, in the Loltún Caves, in the Puuc hills on the Yucatán Peninsula of Mexico, a visitor can learn about the natural and cultural history of the northern Mayan lowlands within a 10,000-year period, from late Pleistocene (1.8 million to 10,000 years ago) to relatively contemporary times. Archaeological excavations have unearthed the remains of antediluvian animals, along with the bones and other material remains—pottery, marine shells, stone artifacts, bas-relief carvings, petroglyphs, and painted murals—that correspond to the distinct developmental stages of Mayan culture, thus making the conclusion that prehistoric creatures coexisted with human beings in the Americas an indisputable scientific fact.

The investigations of Czech anthropologist Aleš Hrdlička (1869–1943), the first scientist to promote the theory of human colonization of the American continent by way of East Asia some 15,000 years ago, and who said that these humans lived in a savage state on this continent, have influenced most subsequent Eurocentric thinking about the origins of humankind. Hrdlička came to the conclusion that "the American and Asiatic aborigines were related from the beginning," and he pointed out characteristics shared by the American and Mongol races, including similarities in skin color, physiognomy, hair, and beards. Fortunately, for the sake of the truth, there have been other researchers who have found evidence to refute Hrdlička's theories: the aforementioned Ameghino brothers, Yucatecan author Ignacio Magaloni Duarte, the great Mexican anthropologist Domingo Martínez Paredes, and Peruvian scholar and physician Javier Cabrera Darquea, to name just a few.

In the deserts of Peru, near the town of Ica, Javier Cabrera Darquea (1924–2001) studied more than 11,000 black stones engraved with cultural depictions that call into question just about everything mainstream science has taught us about the origin of our planet, ourselves, and other species. The engraved andesite stones, called gliptoliths, comprise a sophisticated library left behind by an ancient lost civilization. The images on the stones depict medical transplants and blood transfusions, men with dinosaurs, advanced technology such as telescopes and surgical equipment, the arrangements of lost continents, and space travel. Darquea, a physician who founded the medical school of Ica National University in Peru, spent the last forty years of his life decoding the messages of the stones. He presents significant findings in his book *El mensaje de las piedras grabadas de Ica* (The Recorded Message of the Ica Stones):

> Geology has proven that at the end of the Cretaceous period, the American continent was divided into two continental parts, the south and the north, and no point of union existed between the two; paleontology, for its part, has shown that the fossils of some mammals found in the soil of both continents are the same, but only starting at the beginning of the Tertiary Period (about 63 million years ago), shortly after the epoch in which geology situates the formation of the bridge between the two continents.

So where did such advanced beings as evidenced on the Ica Stones come from? Darquea says they came from the Pleiades, about one million years ago. In fact, the Maya, Inca, Cherokee, and other indigenous peoples of the Americas believe that humankind had galactic origins. These peoples all believe that the seeds of human consciousness originated in

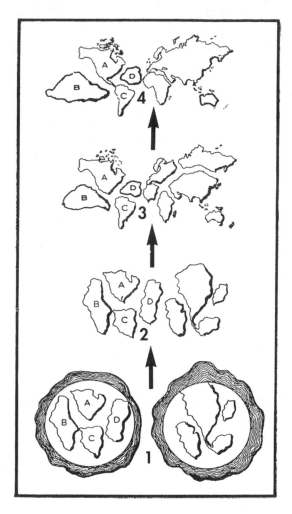

Figure 1.1. Reconstruction of the formation of the world's continents, millions of years ago; read from bottom to top (from Javier Cabrera Darquea's book on the Ica Stones).

Map 1: The beginning of the formation of the world's continents as indicated on the Ica Stones. A indicates what is now North America; B, Lemuria (or Mu); C, what is now South America; D, Atlantis (or Atzantiha).

Map 2: Here the evolution and formation of the continents continues over many millions of years.

Map 3: Here one can begin to see the shapes and positions of the present-day American continents.

Map 4: Here one can see the complete present shape of the Americas. It is estimated that Central America was formed 65 million years ago.

the Pleiades, which was called Tzek'eb by the Maya. According to traditional Mayan belief, our Sun is part of this constellation, and the roots
of humankind can be traced to a time when our ancestors from space
intermingled with the highest form of life on Earth, to bring about the
human being.

That is why throughout Mesoamerica you will find that all the great
temples of the Mayan, Aztec, and Incan cultures were oriented to the
Pleiades. To all these peoples, the many aspects of spirit resonate to the
vibration of the number 7, which represents the Pleiades, the celestial
source of human consciousness. Thus the outer and the inner reflect
each other, in such aspects as the seven inner chakras of the human
being and the outer seven stars of the Pleiades.

The Chilam Balam of Chumayel

The legends and chronicles of the aboriginal peoples of the Americas
transport us back to a time when those who wrote what is known as
"history" did not even exist; they tell of a time when the *wapadz,* or
giant beings, lived. These stories chronicle the knowledge held during
this distant era, in which there was seemingly no known way to count
time. Yet amid these stories we encounter reports of the use of calendars.
So at what period of time were calendars first used in the Americas?

Books today are for us something commonplace; yet for the aboriginal
peoples of times past, the written word was something only a few knew,
and so the written word was at the service of the sacred, because the word
itself was considered sacred. The Maya developed the most complex written language in the Americas; their texts appear in stone, stucco, ceramic,
embroidery; and in sacred papyrus books, or codices. These codices were
records of the spiritual inheritance of the Mayan masters of old—sacred
knowledge that was passed down from generation to generation, destined
to be read in ceremonies of the Maya. The Spanish conquerors said that
these books contained the teachings of the devil; they made it their mission to destroy every last remnant of this great culture, and those who

kept such knowledge were hunted down and killed for practicing crimes against the "true religion" of the Europeans.

For this reason, important Mayan families were entrusted to safeguard the sacred, secret knowledge contained in these books, which were passed down from father to son. Only a few codices survived the bloody Spanish inquisition. They became commonly known as the Dresden, Madrid, Grolier, and Paris codices—because these are the European places where the few surviving books found their way after the Spanish conquest. In addition to these codices, a few texts written after the Spanish inquisition survived: the Popul Vuh of the Quichés, and the sacred books of the Chilam Balam of the Yucatecan Maya.

The Chilam Balam of Chumayel is one of nine books of the Chilam Balam, compiled in the Mayan language by the Yucatecan Maya Juan José Hoil. During the colonial times it was likely passed along to others who participated in the process of interpolating diverse ancient texts as a means of preserving the spiritual legacy of their Yucatecan ancestors, the Maya. The word *chilam* means "that which is mouth" or "that which prophesies." *Balam* means "jaguar" or "wizard"; this is a family name, so *Chilam Balam* refers to a person of the sacred class, a priest, who probably lived some time before the Spanish invasion, and whose gifts of spiritual knowledge included prophecy. This relates to the Mayan conception of time as having a cyclical rhythm, and thus events can be foreseen by certain men of knowledge. The Chilam Balam of Chumayel was cast in the framework of the Mayan calendar and contains specific information on the ancient calendars, their uses, and their cycles. It goes without saying that the reader must make some effort to penetrate the wisdom of this chronicle, which will serve as a portal into our discussion of the Mayan astronomical calendars.

The Chilam Balam of Chumayel tells us: "Thirteen times four hundred times / and fifteen times four hundred times / plus four hundred years of years / the Itzas lived as heretics." Calculating this number of years, we obtain the following quantity: $13 \times 400 = 5200$ years, plus $15 \times 400 = 6000$ years, plus another 400 years. After analyzing these numbers, we come to the conclusion that this is 13 Baktun, 4 Ahau, and 8 Cumhu, the initial date; plus 400 years, making a total of 11,600 years.

According to the traditional Itzae (of which only about 100 elders can still speak the native Itzá Mayan language of old), it was at this time that their ancestors arrived in what is now known as the Yucatán Peninsula of Mexico. The Chilam Balam of Chumayel further says that they came from a place where the waters had swallowed the fount of wisdom, a place that was known in their language as Atzantiha (see figures 1.2 and 1.3). At the time when the Itzae arrived on this continent, these Mayan people were living in a nonsacred manner. Judging by the aforementioned number of years, this may well coincide with the time that geologists date the end of the Ice Age in the Americas. Possibly this Mayan chronicle gives us a more precise figure for the duration of the Ice Age: 11,600 years for glaciation to end and for the northern ice to vanish. According to occultist James Churchward, when the Spanish conquistadors first set foot on the Yucatán they asked the Maya how

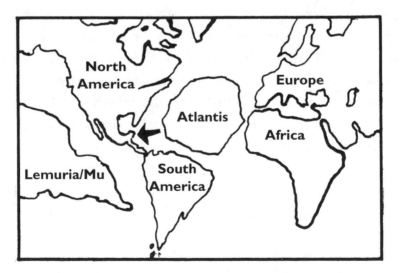

Figure 1.2. Churchward's depiction of the continents before the disappearance of Atlantis and Lemuria (or Mu). According to the Itzae, they came from the east, as the arrow shows. This runs contrary to what mainstream historians claim: namely, that the people who settled the Americas came across the Bering Strait, entering via Alaska.

Figure 1.3. A page from the Mayan Dresden Codex that shows the god Itzamna sailing from the east, where the Maya were said to have come from. They called this place Atzantiha in their Mayan language. It is also worth noting that Itzamna is the symbol of the great Mayan master teacher. His wisdom was the basis for the construction of Ch'iich'en Itzam (usually spelled Chichén Itzá); this initiatory knowledge is manifested in the forms of these temples of the Yucatán.

long they had been living on this land; in response, these people, he says, mentioned the approximate figure of 11,500 years.

After sufficient meditation on the information given by these Mayan dates, we can only conclude that that we cannot agree with the commentaries of mainstream, conventional "scholars," who take great pains to refute the antiquity of the human presence in the Americas, such as Daniel Garrison Brinton, Joseph T. Goodman, and Sylvanus Morley. Most of these Eurocentric investigators can see no farther than the tips of their own noses. They refuse to acknowledge the ancientness of Mesoamerican peoples, in order to prevent the loss of the primacy of man in Europe, Africa, or Asia. According to these scholars, nothing exists in America that is old enough to be considered prehistoric.

It should be noted that the Mayan and Nahua chronicles declare, albeit in a veiled form, that before their ancestors' arrival in these Mesoamerican regions, other peoples had lived here: the people living in Veracruz, Mexico, who were known as the Olmecs. These people were established in the area of what is now the Yucatán, and they left behind many beautiful artifacts of stone and jade, many of which are related to the jaguar. When the Maya arrived in this area, they almost surely found the abandoned pyramids of these earlier residents.

Finally, we should mention the discovery, in 1947, of an early Mesoamerican skeleton, called Tepexpán Man (and who was later discovered to be a woman), in central Mexico, near Mexico City. It has been hypothesized that this individual was crushed beneath the feet of a raging mastodon—in itself sufficient proof that humans lived in very early times on the high plateaus of Mexico, as well as in Central, South, and North America.

The Dresden Codex

A people who had the capability of recording in the written word the phenomena that transformed this planet, as in the Yucatecan Mayan Dresden Codex, could only be a people who would dominate the field of astronomy to the point of perfection. The Dresden Codex, said to be the earliest known book of the Americas (so named because it found its way to Dresden, Germany, after the Spanish conquest—one of the Mayan manuscripts deemed worthy of study by Europeans, no doubt because of its astronomical knowledge) is a folded papyrus book that is assumed to be a later transcription of a much older original. It contains complex calendrical data recorded in the Mayan dating system, including mathematical calculations of planetary movements; it also records which planets interceded to cause the Great Deluge, and the manner in which this affected life on Earth. The standards of perfection to which the Mayan calendar records were held, as exemplified in the observations and calculations contained in this sacred text, are testimony to the exceptional nature of the Mayan culture (see figure 1.4).

1   2   3   4

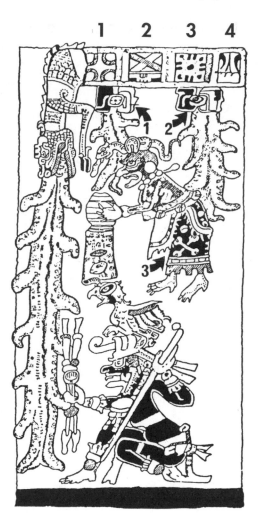

Figure 1.4. In this illustration from the Yucatecan Mayan Dresden Codex, four numbers can be seen in the upper part. The number 1 corresponds to the planet Venus; 2 to Mars; 3 to Mercury; and 4 to Jupiter. This page from the Dresden Codex purports to represent one of the great deluges endured by humanity. A certain condition in our solar system caused the forces of these four planets to conjoin, bringing about a cosmic phenomenon whereby the greater part of the human race was destroyed. Arrow 1 points to a symbol that shows the sun in the center, the day and night on both sides, and below lots of water falling down; arrow 2 points to a symbol that shows the moon in the center and the day and night on both sides, indicating a lunar cycle of twenty-eight days in which it rained a lot; and arrow 3 shows us two bones in the form of an X, indicating that many deaths resulted from so much water falling on the earth.

Atlantis, Lemuria, and the Maya

Let us now consider the theories of inventor, engineer, and occultist James Churchward (1851–1936), who said that in remote times, before the continents of what have been called Atlantis and Lemuria (or Mu) were destroyed, the Maya, Nahua, Hopi, Inca, Aymara, and other peoples who were connected to the lost continents had cultural intercourse that led to the spread of what we know to be Mayan knowledge (see figure 1.5). Churchward explained that Mu, the lost continent of the Pacific, was the origin of civilization, with one branch of colonization that ran to America, and from there to Atlantis.

When considering this map from Churchward, it is important to question whether mainstream historians are telling the truth when they tell us that our aboriginal ancestors came to America by crossing over the Bering Strait into Alaska; likewise when they tell us that Christopher Columbus "discovered" America, or even that our continent should be called the New World. These lies need to be exposed in order to further humanity's cosmic education.

A passage from *Educadores del mundo,* by Maya researcher Ignacio Magaloni Duarte, tells us the following:

> In this study we will show, through the presence of many Mayan radicals in various other languages, that the Mayan language is the ancient mother tongue sought by the world's contemporary philologists. We will then support our proof with important historical facts. . . . The historians of Egypt agree that wise architects came to that land from Atlantis, and taught those people how to carve rocks and build great pyramids.

And from *El Egipto de los faraones* by the historian Juan Marin:

> Horus was part of the Abydos Triad, from which ensued the perfect expression of the triangle and the perfect architectural form

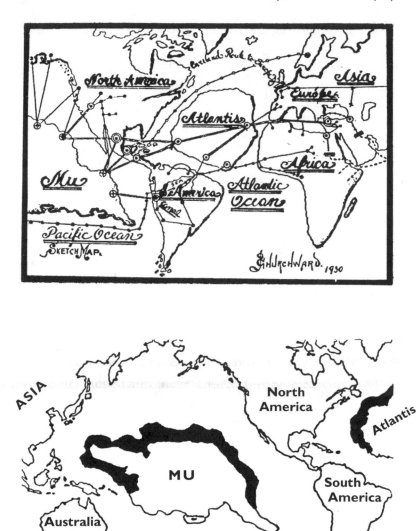

Figure 1.5. James Churchward shows that two continents once existed and later disappeared, having been swallowed by the Pacific and Atlantic oceans. These continents were called Mu (or Lemuria) and Atlantis. As one can see from Churchward's map, the people of Mu were connected to the Maya, Nahua, Hopi, Inca, Aymara, et al., while at the same time all these peoples were connected to Atlantis, which in turn was related to the Egyptians, Ititians, Babylonians, Hindustanis, et al.

of the pyramid. [Horus was the son of Osiris, who was also called great Atlantis] . . . From the archaic sanctuaries of Osiris, we are able to observe and analyze the strange configuration of the puzzling Osirion, a mostly subterranean temple surrounded by canals. The people of this island held the belief that life had emerged in the waters [evolution: a Mesoamerican concept that remained unique for millennia]. This constitutes the symbolic affirmation that Osiris arrived from Atlantis as the first colonist, sent by the sages of that other continent in order to preserve the treasures of science and wisdom in all parts of the world.

According to history, this personage, designer and builder of the six-level step pyramid of Saqqara during the reign of Pharaoh Djoser, 2900 BCE, taught the Egyptians how to cut stone and build pyramids, and was the true father of all the initiatory tradition of the Middle East and medieval Europe. The Osirian Mysteries may be considered as the inspiration for the Orphic and Eleusinian Mysteries that were celebrated in Argos, Phocis, Arcadia, and Mitraikos, and passed from Persia into Armenia, Cappadocia, Sicily, and even Rome.

Egypt and the Maya

To further establish the antiquity of the Mayan civilization and its astronomical calendars, and the connection between Egypt and the Maya, let us now turn to the field of linguistics.

Imhotep was an Egyptian polymath who served under the Third Dynasty pharaoh, Djoser, as chancellor and high priest of the Sun god Ra. An engineer, architect, astrologer, and physician, as well as a patron of scribes who personified wisdom and education, he is considered to have been the architect of the Step Pyramid at Saqqara, in the city of Memphis.

I transcribe the word *Imhotep* as *Inhotep,* with an *n* rather than an *m*. According to my investigations, the Mayan etymology of the word *Inhotep* is: *in,* first-person singular personal pronoun *I;* the next syllable, *ho,* root of the word *hok'ol,* meaning "to emerge"; and, lastly, the syllable *tep,* root of the word *tepeu.* This word is clearly explained in the Popol Vuh, which tells us that Tepeu and Gugumatz (i.e., Kukulcán) were the creators, or molders, of humans, through the power given them by Hunab K'u, the Absolute One. And so to summarize this analysis: *Inhotep* means "I emerge as the Creator." The Egyptians considered him one of their masters and accorded him divine status after his death. Now look at figure 1.6 (on page 20), which shows the pyramids of Kukulcán, in Mexico, and Saqqara, in Egypt. Note the distinct similarity in the structures of both.

As I noted in my book *Secrets of Mayan Science/Religion,* the historian-priest of Babylonia, Berosus the Chaldean, told how the Maya arrived in his homeland, descending in the form of fish, bringing their culture; and Manetho, the Egyptian priest, historian, and mathematician, maintained that the Maya lived in Atlantis for 13,900 years. Many other historians, priests, and philosophers attributed to the Maya a significant role in bringing culture to their parts of the world.

Investigator Pedro Guirao, in his book *Mu, ¿Paraíso Perdido?,* adds to the body of research that confirms the antiquity of the Mayan civilization, as well as its connection with that of Egypt:

Augusto Le Plongeon, in his work entitled *La Reina Moo y la Esfinge Egipcia* [*Queen Moo and the Egyptian Sphinx*], published in New York in 1900, as well as James Churchward claim that the last sovereign of the Can dynasty, Queen Moo, visited the Mayan colony located in Egypt, near the Nile River, during the first century of its existence; this took place around 16,000 years ago. They also tell us that the Sphinx is the effigy of Queen Moo, built to commemorate this important visit.

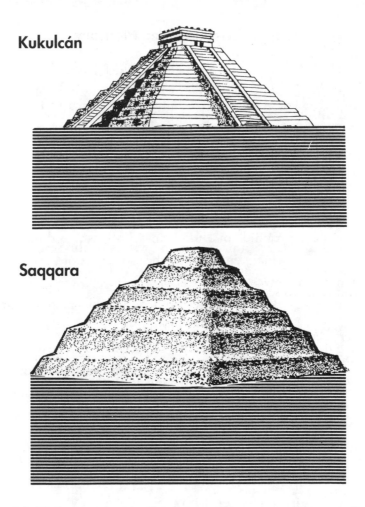

Kukulcán

Saqqara

Figure 1.6. The two pyramids, Kukulcán and Saqqara, exhibit an indisputable similarity in their architecture; it is also possible that the ritual and scientific use of each structure was oriented toward a common purpose. The upper pyramid is Kukulcán, in Chichén Itzá, Yucatán, Mexico; the lower pyramid is the Step Pyramid of Saqqara, in Egypt. The construction of this latter pyramidal monument is attributed to Inhotep, architect of Pharaoh Djoser, the same person to whom the art of construction in stone is attributed. The name of Inhotep is engraved in a statue near the tomb of Pharaoh Djoser. The wisdom of Inhotep became legendary, since he also taught medicine, astronomy, and magic. The Greeks identified him with medicine, and later even replaced the name Inhotep with that of Asclepius, thus establishing his identity as the god of medicine. Inhotep built the Step Pyramid of Saqqara on an elevated strip of land that divided the city. The Egyptians relate that even more than 1,000 years after the Pyramid of Saqqara was built, the perfection of its architecture continued to be admired.

Mayan Cosmic Solar Memory

Today we have forgotten how to remember, which has to do with all the bad education that was imposed on us human beings during thousands of years of different forms of colonialism. As a Maya, I can remember with my cosmic mind. And you also, kind reader, can begin to learn to remember with your cosmic mind, because you, too, are a cosmic being.

In a long-ago world age, before the Maya arrived in the sacred lands in which we now live, they were in many lands that can no longer be seen physically, that are now under the waters of the sea. They traveled to many places, as did many other native human beings, like the Hopi, who came to settle in what is today known as the United States of America, at a time when many parts of that land were still under the sea. In very remote times the Maya lived in high mountains, in places with a lot of ice; they were also in desert lands that eventually were transformed, some into bigger lands, some into small islands.

The Maya can remember the continent of Lemuria, or Lemulia, as it is known in the Mayan language, a place where their cosmic religion was understood and practiced. Many different peoples inherited the sacred symbols of Lemulia, which represented the summation of wisdom. One of these symbols is what is known as the Star of David of the Hebrews.

The old Itzae, as our ancestors of tradition were known, can remember when we were living on the continent of Atlantis, or Atlantiha in the Mayan language. For thousands of years we lived in this land, where our sacred religious symbols were deposited. Those who lived there in many communities could understand the cosmic wisdom that had been deposited, and here arose more sacred symbols that were part of universal wisdom, and part of this people's cosmic education. When their cosmic wisdom, as revealed through their calendars, indicated that a cycle would come to an end, many of these communities emigrated to other places of magnetic power, taking their spiritual and scientific knowledge with them to new lands. The sacred teachings from the cosmos were thus deposited in many magnetic centers throughout the world: Chan Chan (Peru), Huete (Spain), Tulle (France), Hu-nan (China), Bethlehem (Israel), Tih (Egypt), Mississippi (United States), Humac (Brazil), Nagasaki (Japan), Mul (England), Maya (Russia), and Naga (India), to name a few. The names of all these places are of Mayan origin.

To understand the great law of Hunab K'u, my ancestors, the ancient Maya, visited all of these places. They traveled to all the cardinal points, North, South, East, and West. When they arrived in the province of Shensi, a group of pyramids was built there, one of them rising 300 meters. When they were in Tibet, the great white pyramid located along the Himalaya mountain range was built. In the forests of Cambodia the pyramid of Angkor was built. All these pyramidal temples, and those in Egypt and other places, were built when humans lived in the light of cosmic wisdom.

This great continent that is known as America was known by the Itzae of tradition as Tamaunchan. And thus arose Tamaunchan as a continuation of the cosmic spiritual education of the people. Those who came here brought with them the knowledge of Atlantiha, but in the new land of Tamaunchan they developed still more spiritual knowledge together with the inhabitants of these new lands, who became known as the Maya. In this manner, the Maya inherited the knowledge of Atlantihas and developed still more cosmic wisdom. And they created with their sacred language the Mayan words *Hunab K'u,* which for them represented the great concept of the creation of the universe.

2

HUNAB K'U: GIVER OF
MOVEMENT AND MEASURE

The ancient Maya shared with other indigenous peoples of Mesoamerica a highly developed sense of intuitive reasoning, free will, and fierce perseverance in service to the truth. For these Mayan masters, science was not separate from religion or philosophy; they applied logic to Panche Be, the search for the root of truth. The Mayan sages exhaustively observed nature; not only did they devote themselves to interpreting Mother Earth and all her manifestations in nature, but they accorded equal diligence to the observation of the movements and positions of the celestial bodies in infinite space—which is how they achieved such precise scientific knowledge in the disciplines of astronomy and astrology. Their astronomical calendars were the result of their search, and they are what led them to understand the cycles of cosmic time so perfectly.

As a result of their impeccable observations, the Maya concluded that they themselves were part of nature. But instead of a mythical concept of "gods," as found, for example, in the Greek myths, the Mayan philosopher-scientists maintained that the different lords represented the different forces of nature. Being part of nature, they further deduced that they shared a common element with everything in nature: a soul.

For the Maya, the soul was perceived as having material form, since everything in nature has form. This is distinct from spirit, which for the Maya was pure energy, or *k'inan,* which comes from the word for the Sun, *K'in,* with the suffix *an,* a conditional form of the verb *to be.* K'inan—spirit-energy, or the solar factor—is thus spirit; soul, then, is the manifestation of spirit, a conduit of spirit. This deduction, which was the simple truth for the Maya, has been something that modern science has only just begun to recognize: that even the tiniest components of matter conform to certain geometric patterns whose dimensions are maintained by an intelligent energy—an energy that fuels all human intellectual and creative activity.

And what is the source of this intelligent energy? Through a process of logic and synthesis, and a high level of conceptual understanding, the Mayan philosopher-scientists came to the conclusion that there is an absolute being. But their definition of the absolute being was not a god with a defining personality, like the biblical God the Spanish invaders later tried to impose on this advanced Mayan people. Nor was it a distant, separate being, off in a faraway "kingdom of heaven" looking "down" on creation. No, the Mayan supreme being was found to be a unity with humans and all things of nature, and was expressed in terms of a mathematical component: the measure of the soul and the movement of the energy that is spirit—the universal dynamism that stimulates and motivates life in its manifestation of spirit and matter; the principle of intelligent energy that pervades the entire universe, animate or inanimate.

This being so, the Mayan sages could only conclude that each individual human being was one with every other being—that the unity of human with human was, in fact, the true nature of the human being—and that human beings were, in fact, one with all things of nature. They embraced the microcosm of the atom and the macrocosm of the infinite, the spiritually evolved concept of plurality in unity, unity in plurality.

From this standpoint, it was only logical for the Maya to deduce that the "gods" (i.e., the forces of nature), humans, and numbers were one and the same, and that all were expressions of Hunab K'u: the architect of the universe. This God, this supreme energy, of which all things of nature are but manifestations, was called the Giver of Movement as well as the Giver of Measure, because *there can be no movement that does not have measure.* Knowing that God is energy, and energy is God, the Mayan philosopher-scientists established the oneness of human beings with Hunab K'u, who is communicated numerically as the union of the numbers 13 and 20, which represent movement and measure, energy and form, soul and spirit. This numerical representation is found in the geometric form of a square within a circle—a synthesis of universal geometry based on the human body.

Sacred Geometry: The Circle and the Square

Because geometry was at the basis of their reasoning, the Maya used it to represent the supreme architect and creator of the universe, Hunab K'u: the intelligent energy that palpably demonstrates its wisdom via its chronological laws, guiding the material things of this world. One of the proofs of this fact is the Mayan word *men,* which means "to create, to form, to make"; the mental force that feeds intelligence and gives us the capacity to know, understand, and comprehend, in order to be able to invent or discover, by means of our intelligence, the divine gift that the supreme architect of the universe has bestowed on human beings.

Let us probe more deeply into this discussion of the Giver of Movement and Measure by examining what anthropologist Domingo Martínez Paredes tells us regarding Pythagoras and numbers, in Maestro Paredes' essay "Hunab K'u, Synthesis of Mayan Philosophic Thought":

For both the Pythagoreans and the Maya, numbers were held sacred. Pythagoras taught that the number 12 was the infinite, while the Maya, for their part, believed the number 13 to be the infinite, since a meaning had already been given to 12: this number represented the 12 deities who guarded the corners of the heavens, the ideal boundaries within which all the things of life take place.

Pythagoras conceived of the number 5 as the vital order, and the Maya considered it so as well; it represented no less than the solar path, the greatest expression of the omnipresence of Hunab K'u— the Bearer of Movement and Measure—revered at 2 solstices and 2 equinoxes, plus the central point of the sun, totaling 5. Likewise, he was represented as the human torso, with the two cavities from which the arms rotate, the two joints of the legs, and the navel as the center.

If the Pythagoreans claimed that all things are numbers and that the world is formed by numbers, the Maya, for their part, determined that all things are realized through the course of thirteen numbers, and are subject to two fundamental geometric figures: the circle and the square, or the spherical and cubic forms.

Not only do we find similarities in the thinking of the Greeks and the Maya concerning sacred numbers and geometric forms; there are also strong parallels in how the Egyptians and the Maya and the Teotihuacános thought of numbers and geometric forms, as can be seen in figure 2.1. (Recall in chapter 1 Pedro Guirao's statement that the Maya were in Egypt some 16,000 years ago.) To continue with this examination of the parallels to Mayan culture, here again is Maestro Paredez:

Recall the similarity existing between certain Christian practices and those of the Maya, such as baptism, confession, etc. But the greatest coincidence, and what made such a strong impression on the Spaniards, was the existence of a being who was the eternal father, on whom everything depended, even including Christ, his son. Thus, faced with such a manifestation of omnipotence, omnipresence, and omniscience, the Spaniards could hold no doubt that Hunab K'u was the same as their own God.

For their part, the conquering Spaniards, upon learning of the existence of Hunab K'u, did not hesitate in their thinking that this must be

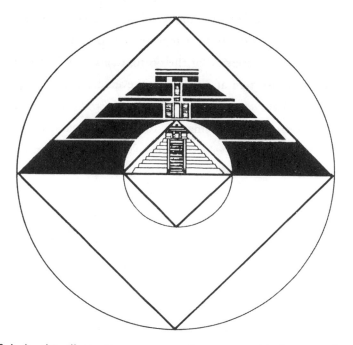

Figure 2.1. In this illustration, we see three pyramids integrated within a circle and a square. The first, the smallest, is the Pyramid of Kukulcán, in Chichén Itzá; the middle one is the Pyramid of the Sun, in Teotihuacán; and the third is the Pyramid of Cheops, in Egypt. As one can see, the geometric outline used for the construction of these three pyramids was the circle and the square.

Hunab K'u, the one held sacred by the Maya and represented geometrically by the circle and the square, is integrated into all three pyramids, which were built in different places, at great distances from one another, but interconnected by a common concept that is inherent to sacred geometry. That no one should doubt this, we note that the builders of all three pyramids used not only the same science, but also the same terminology: the true name of the Egyptian pyramid known as Cheops is K'ufu; the name of the Mayan pyramid is K'u; the words *K'u* and *K'ufu* come from the same language.

the same supreme Creator as their own. How else to explain the Mayan adoration of the cross? Culturally, the Spaniards could never grasp the truly profound metaphysical meaning that the cross held for the Maya: a transcendental synthesis of Mayan religious experience.

The ancient Mayan word for tree is *te,* from the words *teol* and *teotl* as the names of God the Creator in the Mayan and Nahuatl languages, and is symbolized by the letter *T*. It represents spirit, wind, or the divine breath. The Sacred Tree, or Tree of Life, which is also called the Axis Mundi or Universal Axis, is the connection to the spirit world as well as the connection between heaven and earth. This most revered word of the ancient people, symbolized in the Sacred Tree, a symbol of the supreme architect, was represented in Mayan hieroglyphs and in all forms of indigenous architecture in the Americas, as in the T-shaped doorway or window and in the form of the cross. There is no religion in the world that does not use this symbol in conjunction with the cosmobiological laws to which we are subject—the Tree of Life being, for the Maya, the portal connecting to Hunab K'u. Whenever this symbol was used in Mayan rituals and ceremonies, the Mayan people were reuniting themselves with their true origins.

In distant times and ages past, the sacred Tree of Life was one of the symbols taken by the Maya to the people of Asia, Africa, and Europe. With the passage of time, these symbols returned to us with the Spanish conquistadors, but by then this symbol, and others, carried a distorted message of its sacred content, to refer to the suffering of human beings. The conquered Mayan people wept like babies when the Spanish friars exhibited their cross bearing the bloody, crucified body of Jesus, who taught love, generosity, and affection for one's neighbor, much like the Mayan expression *In Lak'ech* (You are me and I am you); they clearly could not understand why a symbol of unique goodness and power could be used to torture someone! For their part, the Spaniards couldn't figure out what was bothering the Maya; clearly this was an example of the misuse of symbols—in this case, the cross.

No, there was no doubt on the part of the Spaniards that some Christian apostle had passed through these Mayan lands; they even came to the conclusion that the Aztec Quetzalcoatl, the Feathered Serpent who is the sacred energy that gives perpetual life to the cosmos, known to the Maya as Kukulcán, had been Saint Thomas himself. Martínez Paredes continues:

We say this because this influence of Hunab K'u, under the names of Tonalpohuaque and Ipalnemohuani ["He by whom the people live"], worshipped by the Aztec people, extended through all of what was then called New Spain, and had begun to rise above the ruins of the Old Anahuac, just as the Catholic religion of Christ had displaced the mathematical concept of God as the Unique Bearer of Movement and Measure, inscribed in the magic of the geometric forms and numbers.

In Tloke Nahuake and Ipalnemohuani were the names of the Sacred One for the Mexicas and Aztecs at the time the Spanish conquistadors arrived in Mesoamerica. This Supreme Being, the Bearer of Movement and Measure, is the same one that the Maya of the Yucatán worshipped, Hunab K'u, and was similarly represented in the Aztec calendar as a circle and the square—the synthesis of the universal concept of the sacred, represented geometrically.

Even up to the present day, it is still not known how many thousands of years the Maya paid homage to the architect of the universe, magnificently represented by these two geometric forms. It is very important to note that when the Itzae first arrived in the Yucatán, they mentioned that these lands had been submerged in the ocean many times before. This means that the Mayan people had recorded in their astronomical calendars all the ages in which the Yucatán Peninsula had sunk beneath the sea, so their memory was very great.

Hence catastrophic cultural damage, for both the Maya and the rest of humanity, was wrought during the Spanish conquest when the invaders instigated huge massacres and unwittingly spread many diseases to which the native people had no immunity. Those who survived the conquest learned to mask their ancient gods in the symbolism of the Christian saints, just as they learned to use the Roman alphabet as a way of concealing their sacred texts. Then, in 1562, the Spanish friar Diego de Landa launched a bloody inquisition when he discovered the Maya were concealing their innumerable sacred writings, or codices, of their ancestors' knowledge—writings that he could not comprehend yet labeled "diabolical." Fray Landa tortured countless Maya, burned 224 Mayan codices, and destroyed more than 5,000 statues and tablets—the Mayan civilization's vast library of cosmic knowledge and the history of the world, as well its legacy of the sciences, literature, philosophy, and religion. As a result of Fray Landa's inquisition, the Maya were forced to keep their knowledge secret, within their families; you would have been killed by the inquisition otherwise. My family kept twelve generations of this knowledge in secret. My uncle was a shaman, and before he died he passed the sacred knowledge on to me.

For these reasons, when investigating the Mayan people and other ancient peoples of the Americas, we must look beyond the errors and oversights made by those who have distorted information about the indigenous peoples of Mesoamerica and denied their culture, like the Eurocentric scholars Daniel Garrison Brinton, Joseph T. Goodman, Charles Pickering Bowditch, Sylvanus Morley, and Aleš Hrdlička, who are simply ignorant about our culture. Then there are the new breed of fantasist writers, who use their imaginations to distort reality, like Erich von Däniken, author of *Chariots of the Gods,* who proposes space-ship origins for Mayan culture and in saying this, annihilates our true Mesoamerican roots.

To prove the past glory of Mesoamerica and to demonstrate its validity, we should consider the indigenous Arahuaco of Colombia, among whom the shaman Crispín Izquierdo resides. This shaman knows Hunab K'u well; in fact, it was he who imparted the geometric wisdom of the Arahuaco people to me when I visited there, as can be seen in figures 2.2 and 2.3.

According to this shaman, figure 2.2(a) symbolizes the Father of Thought; (b) the Mother of Fertility; and (c) the Father and Mother, or the Sacred Ones, of Planet Earth. Here we should take into account that for the Arahuaco, "Father and Mother" means something slightly differ-ent than the reversed order, "Mother and Father." For them, when the order changes, the teaching also changes, as we will see in the discussion that follows, since "Father" represents the Sacred One, and "Mother" means Mother Earth. Next, figure 2.2(d), for the Arahuaco, is the representation of the three levels of which we individual human beings are a microcosm: (1) Earth, (2) cosmos, and (3) the infinite. These three circles also have corresponding colors: black for Earth, white for the cosmos, and yellow and red for the infinite.

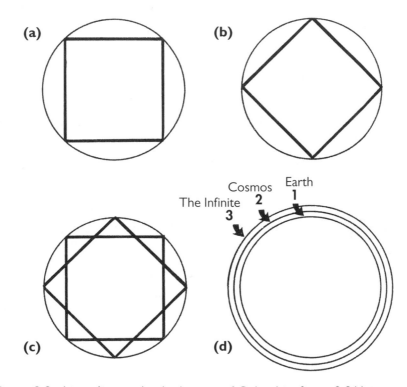

Figure 2.2. According to the Arahuacos of Colombia, figure 2.2(a) represents the Father of Thought; (b) represents the Mother of Fertility, who is the mother of Planet Earth; and (c) represents the Father and Mother of Planet Earth, or the Sacred Ones of Planet Earth. The two interlaced squares represent the union of the Father and Mother, of the macrocosm and the microcosm, and this union can be found in all existing things. In figure 2.2(d), the inner circle represents Earth, the middle circle represents the cosmos, and the outer circle represents the infinite. According to the Arahuaco people, contemporary science is on the level of Earth, and has hardly even begun to see the cosmic level. For science to see the infinite level, it must begin to work in the spiritual domain. Only in this manner will it be possible to see the superior level that is the infinite.

In figure 2.3(a), the vertical line symbolizes the Father and the horizontal line the Mother. When the vertical line points upward, it is oriented toward the Father, or male; when it points downward, it is oriented toward the Mother, or female. These two lines together symbolize the human being. According to the Arahuaco sages, the place where they intersect is where the center of the human being is to be found: namely, at the navel. Figure 2.3(b) shows us the Father and Mother of equilibrium of all existence, and this form is present in all human beings. The Arahuaco sages add that when this form fails within us, we are in danger of being injured by the Father and Mother of equilibrium. Figure 2.3(c) shows us how the Father and Mother leave the human being. With this illustration, the indigenous Arahuaco sages give us a warning: we humans must maintain this equilibrium, or sacred form, which according to them is present in many places, but principally in all the pyramids of the world, which are libraries of cosmic wisdom and cosmic consciousness that serve as portals to those dimensions when visited by human beings. Finally, figure 2.3(d), according to the Arahuaco masters, is the perfect form, which governs all existence on Earth, in the cosmos, and in the infinite; it also governs the human being, mathematics, geometry, the sacred, and the cycles of time (or, to put it more accurately, the calendars). Very little is yet known of this wisdom of the indigenous Arahuaco people, but there is a great deal that we can learn from them.

In analyzing this series of profound teachings and the entire cosmogonic and geometric concepts of our Arahuaco brothers in Colombia, we arrive at the conclusion that this wisdom is the same as that of the Mayan Hunab K'u, and the same as the Aztec/Mexicas wisdom of In Tloke Nahuake and Ipalnemohuani; and it is the same sacred teaching represented by geometry, mathematics, and the cosmos. This is magnificently depicted by the Arahuaco masters of Colombia in figure 2.4. And so in this manner, the Egyptians, Teotihuacános, Nahua, Maya, Terbis, Arahuaco, Inca, Aymara, et al., are united as the educators of humanity.

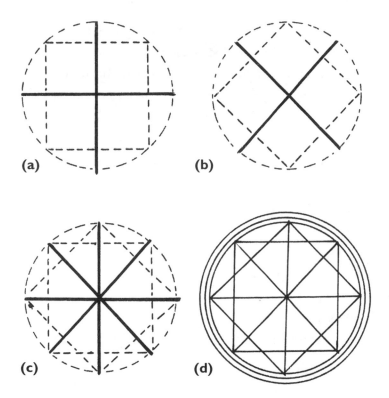

Figure 2.3. These geometric forms are a continuation of the teachings of the Arahuaco masters of Colombia. Figure 2.3(a) shows us the Father by means of a vertical line directed upward, and when the line points downward, it indicates the Mother, or Goddess of the Earth. The horizontal line symbolizes the Mother. In figure 2.3(b), the two lines in an X indicate the Father and Mother of equilibrium, present in all existence. Figure 2.3(c) shows the Father and Mother and the emergence of the human being from this geometric form; it also illustrates the Arahuaco maxim that the human being is responsible for maintaining this form in order for equilibrium to remain. Figure 2.3(d), according to the Arahuaco masters, represents the fact that human beings must live in harmony with one another and with all that surrounds them for this form to maintain perfect equilibrium.

As we penetrate further into this analysis of the Mayan astronomical calendars, we must pay special attention to figure 2.4, which shows Hunab K'u integrated into his geometric representation. This diagram is fundamental to understanding the Mayan calendars and Hunab K'u as the Bearer of Movement and Measure. If the students of the

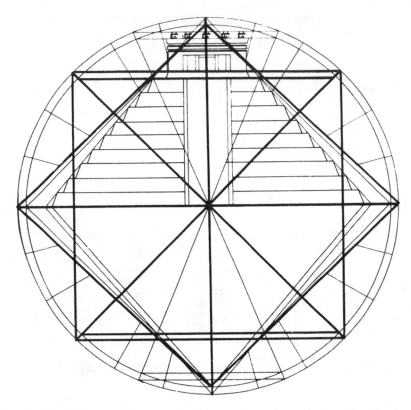

Figure 2.4. All that was previously mentioned regarding the Arahuaco teachings in the previous illustrations can be seen in this drawing, in which we can also see the Pyramid of Kukulcán, the sacred symbol of the Mayan people, inside the circle and square. Using this geometric form—the circle, square, and lines—the Mayan people represented the synthesis of the philosophical thought of this great, ancestral, continentwide culture, the Mother and Father of so many other cultures of the world. For the Maya, the circle and square were the symbol of the Sacred One, Hunab K'u, who rules all physical and spiritual existence. Hunab K'u already existed when all things were suspended in calm, in silence, when the void was the extent of the heavens, when nothing was yet manifest on Earth. Thus were all things when Hunab K'u first existed, pervading everything.

Pythagorean school had read this book, it is certain that the school's alumni would never have forgotten the symbol of this geometric form! This form confirms that God, numbers, and geometry all serve the highest teaching; they are all one.

The Prevalence of Hunab K'u
in Architecture

This discussion of the circle and the square should not pass without mentioning that Hunab K'u's representation in the form of mathematical measurements and geometric forms has been integrated into the architecture of all the native peoples on the continent of Tamuanchan, or America, who have not been culturally assimilated by European colonizers. For example, in Luis Ferrero's book *Costa Rica Precolombina,* one may read about the construction of a house by the indigenous Terbi people, in which the geometric form of the Mayan Hunab K'u is clearly visible: the Sacred One is represented by a circle and a square, since these two shapes represent movement and measure. For a better understanding, see figure 2.5 (page 36).

That the Supreme One is manifest in the geometry of all the calendar pyramids and other sacred sites that store higher knowledge and the history of our continent—confirming the Mayan belief that the calendars tell us of God's cyclical changes—goes without saying. Scattered across the jungles of the Yucatán and the highlands of what is today called Guatemala are incredible numbers of ancient cities and temples, towering stepped pyramids, finely designed plazas, and ceremonial centers completely adorned with sculpture and inscribed with hieroglyphic messages.

Among the Inca of Peru, there are many fine examples of sacred architecture throughout that land, such as at Ollantaytambo, sixty kilometers northwest of the city of Cusco. Here one finds the sacred geometry of Hunab K'u in various temples and in the defenses, which were built by the emperor Manco Inca to fend off attacks by the Spanish conquistadors. These people understood that all that is manifest, animate and inanimate, is merely a projection of energy, of God, and so they employed the concept of universal geometry in their traditional architecture, depicting the circle and square, thus sealing their conviction that God is energy, that energy is God. Modern science, such as

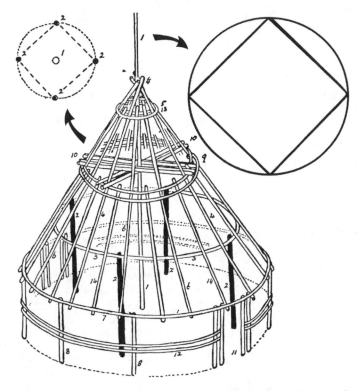

Figure 2.5. Reconstruction of the framework of this type of house, from the book *Costa Rica Precolombina* by Luis Ferrero. According to the indigenous point of view, this architectural drawing is much more than a simple plan for a house. For the Maya it is in the construction that the comprehension of the sacred begins, namely the god Hunab K'u, whom we all worship. Our God is integrated into the structure of our traditional houses. For this reason, when nighttime comes, according to true Mayan culture, we ask Hunab K'u to receive our bodies and spirits and to watch over us as we sleep. We do this because we know that he is with us in our house; in turn, we know this because the sacred element is integrated architecturally and geometrically into the construction of our houses.

quantum physics, also understands this concept, but the difference is that science has only just begun to contemplate this fact; the Maya and other native peoples were never ignorant of it. In making the concept of God mathematical, the Maya and other traditional peoples synthesized universal geometry and therefore knew that nothing exists outside of movement and measure.

3

FORMS OF THE
CALENDARS IN MESOAMERICA

Imagine, dear reader, the night sky in our Mayan ancestors' time, before the ubiquitous artificial lights of the so-called civilized modern world. At night the Mayan adepts could view the depths of the universe, the stars as bright and near as if they were part of the landscape, even merging with the horizon, until vanishing over the edge with a flicker. To the Maya of old, the universe was not a mere concept or a pale abstraction, but a matter of direct experience. The celestial bodies governed the rhythm of life completely, such that time, perceived in terms of the Sun, the Moon, planets, and stars, was experienced as the ever-present, ever-recurring, self-renewing *movement* that is the essence of all existence. The Mayan sages said that the essence of all of creation is movement, i.e., change, vibration. If a creation should ever cease to change its position, or its vibration, that creation ceases to exist.

The adept Mayan sky watchers spent thousands of years of careful observation of the celestial dome. Their calendars were the result of their tenacious recording of the constant movements of the celestial bodies. This very precise mathematical knowledge of the planets and their cycles can be said to have formed the basis of their spiritual culture, because the pulsations of Hunab K'u were understood to be conveyed through the language of the celestial energies and their corresponding mathematical codes. The Maya, along with other Mesoamerican peoples who developed similar calendars, came to the conclusion that everything is in constant movement. From this they deduced that the key to understanding all things mathematical is the calendar, because time rules all things. That is why the Mesoamerican peoples developed various calendars for various purposes. And this is why calendars were ever-present in their lives, in myriad forms and shapes, and not just in the monumental forms: the calendars manifested in the everyday, commonplace things of life. Only in Mesoamerica has there been such an emphasis on observing the cyclic nature of time, and only here has there been such a preponderance of calendars (see figure 3.1). Thus when most of the calendars of the ancient ones were destroyed by the Spanish, humanity suffered a grievous loss. Needless to say, this is why Mesoamerican wisdom was never known, let alone understood, by Europeans.

Fortunately, the Spaniards were not able to complete their total destruction of this millenarian knowledge contained in the Mesoamerican calendars. Today humanity has a great opportunity to learn from the calendars that are left to us, for they contain cosmic knowledge that can bring humanity back into the correct alignment with the natural rhythms of creation. Why is this so? *Because our relationship with nature is connected to our perception of time.* The unnatural timing of the Gregorian calendar system—described by José Argüelles in *Time and the Technosphere* as "artificial time"—which does not synchronize with any natural cycle, serves only to disempower human beings by obscuring their natural connection to nature, the cosmos, and Hunab K'u. This forces humanity into the abyss of physical and spiritual destruction by a few groups that control the majority of humankind—all of which amounts to a conspiracy against the human race and Mother Nature.

The whole of humanity today needs the education coming from the cosmos, because, as it is known, the education of modern civilization is not complying with the universal Creator's correct educational mandates. Many times it contradicts it without understanding it. Today we have an imposed civilization personified by humanity's manipulators. Only the wisdom of the new cosmic time will correct that which

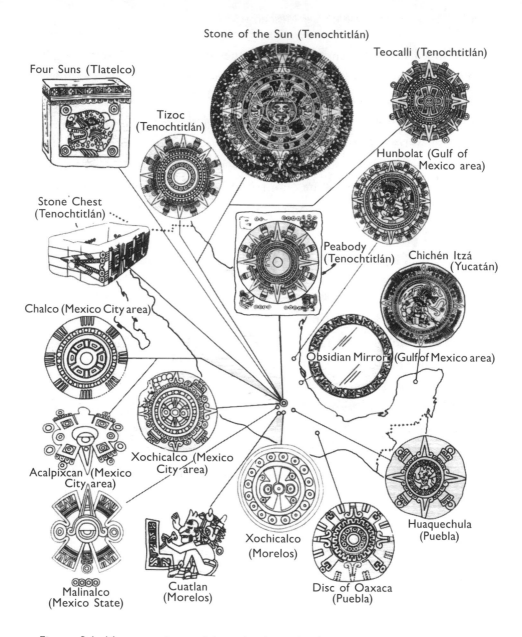

Stone of the Sun (Tenochtitlán)

Teocalli (Tenochtitlán)

Four Suns (Tlatelco)

Tizoc (Tenochtitlán)

Hunbolat (Gulf of Mexico area)

Stone Chest (Tenochtitlán)

Peabody (Tenochtitlán)

Chichén Itzá (Yucatán)

Chalco (Mexico City area)

Obsidian Mirror (Gulf of Mexico area)

Acalpixcan (Mexico City area)

Xochicalco (Mexico City area)

Huaquechula (Puebla)

Malinalco (Mexico State)

Cuatlan (Morelos)

Xochicalco (Morelos)

Disc of Oaxaca (Puebla)

Figure 3.1. Mesoamerica and its calendars. At this time it is necessary for every thinking human being to understand the Mayan astronomical calendars because they point out the code by which the pulsations of Hunab K'u are known, so that human beings can commence their cosmic education and our planet can be restored to harmony with the natural and cosmological cycles. Here are the names of seventeen, among what undoubtedly were many more, calendars that exist in Mesoamerica; the rest are now lost to us (drawing from Hugh Harleston Jr.'s *El Misterio de las Pirámides de Mexico*).

has been badly done; only the great creative forces of the cosmos and of Mother Earth will correct the mistaken road that was imposed on humanity. Only Hunab K'u will disturb 2,000 years of mistaken direction and eradicate these thousands of years of darkness. That is why these Mayan calendars must be newly evaluated. Only once the so-called First World understands these astronomical calendars and their implications for human beings will it attain the status of a truly civilized culture.

The Tonal Machiotl, or Stone of the Sun

When discussing the calendars used in Mesoamerica, it is essential to mention the master engineer Esteban Serieys with all the respect he merits. During his lifetime, Master Serieys taught people about the calendars and their uses. We hope with all our hearts that Hunab K'u is now holding him in sacred glory, and that he will continue to send us his vibration of wisdom from the great beyond. We must now draw from the font of scientific and philosophical observations he made regarding the Aztec Calendar, or Stone of the Sun, which he referred to by its Nahuatl name as the Tonal Machiotl (see figure 3.2). Though prominent scholars and historians, both Mexican and foreign, have devoted their efforts to investigating this magnificent monument to the Mesoamerican culture, they have been unable to decipher its true meaning. Nonetheless, their work has achieved some appreciable results with regard to the numerical symbols, which, partially deciphered, allow us to come to certain conclusions. With the kind permission of Master Serieys, I now reproduce here some of the notes I made while attending his lectures on the Tonal Machiotl.

Contrary to what is stated by Mexican and foreign researchers such as Sahagun, Alaman, Seller, and Herman Bayer, the stone is *not* precisely a calendar (as the last two claim), nor is it a simple piece of engraved stone. It is a monument with inscriptions and chronological information, unique throughout the world, a synthesis of cultures that were incredibly advanced in the realm of the sciences of chronology, astronomy, and mathematics.

These aforementioned scholars focused not on the entire schematic content of the stone, but only on the second circle, in which hieroglyphs have been discovered that correspond to seven of the twenty days that formed the structure of the Aztec month. These are inscribed in the ritual calendar that is known as Tonalpohualli, and which was used principally to indicate complete planetary periods. For this reason, the second circle is identical in its purpose to the squares or tables of planetary revolutions in modern cosmogonies.

The manipulation of the planetary-celestial pattern by the Mesoamerican peoples was not the result of chance, but of minute records that were made in the form of a chronological sequence of transcendental events and observations that always related to the past of human beings on this planet and the direct interrelating of their behavior with the natural elements of the surrounding area, under direct cosmic influence.

The construction of this monument was the result of the Great Astronomical Congress of Tenochtitlán, which was held in Cholula, Puebla, Mexico, due to favorable cosmic conditions, in the [Gregorian] year 1479. In the area surrounding this consecrated site, one can still admire the carvings that the participating astronomer-priests—Zapotec, Olmec, and Mayan, among others—brought from their lands: tablets containing records of the times and places at which events were celebrated.

Under the direct supervision of Tlahtoani Atzayaclat, the primary construction of the monolith began, and afterward, the erection of the stone itself. The ceremony to inaugurate the monument took place two years later, in [Gregorian year] 1481, at which time the stone was put in place, lying horizontally, at the center of a circular site twenty fathoms around.

For the celebration of the stone's dedication, the following peoples were invited: the tecuhtli (dignitaries or lords); the friendly peoples, and principally among them the Huexotzingo, Cholollan, Tlazcala, and Metztitlán; and the popular representations of the deities Quetzalcoatl, Tlaloc, Opochtli, Izpapalotl, Yohualahua, Apantecutli, Huitzilopochtli, Toci, Cihuacoatl, Izquitecatl, Yenopilli, Mixcoatl, and Tepuztecatl, who together number 13, a sacred number that also holds chronological significance.

This stone is a marvel, not only because of its magnificent carved reliefs, but also because of its size. Due to its weight of twenty-two tons, and its dimensions of 3.70 × 3.90 meters, it must have been incredibly difficult to transport with the means available at the time. It is curious to note that the exact diameter of the carving is 3.57 meters, which, multiplied by 88—the number of days it takes the planet Mercury to revolve around the sun—yields 314.16, a figure that in turn, when divided by 100, yields the transcendental number 3.1416, which, of course, is pi. This number, along with the many others that can be obtained from the combinations of glyphs and positions, demonstrates the advanced science and mathematics behind the design—an extraordinary level of technology for the epoch.

The name Cuauhxicalli, by which this stone is officially known by the INAH (Instituto Nacional de Antropología e Historia), was chosen by the Jesuit scholar Juan Eusebio Nieremberg (1595–1658), who described the seventy-eight edifices of the Great Plaza of Tenochtitlán, along with their locations, in his book on this subject. [Note: Because Nieremberg's work, based on the accounts of Spanish missionaries, supposedly includes the indigenous names for things, it became an ersatz linguistic document of the Nahuatl and Quechua languages.] Nieremberg described the eighth building as a house, which he called Cuauhxicalco; by his own decision, without consulting any experts, he located our stone there, along with the number that indicates its position. We consider this absurd given the translation in Nahuatl: *cuauhtli,* "eagle," and *xicalli,* "vessel," thus gives the meaning "vessel of the eagles," or the recipient of the blood of those who were sacrificed, according to the reports of various friars who considered themselves historians and chroniclers of Mesoamerican culture—and all of which runs contrary to the scientific and true significance of the monument.

This stone, positioned horizontally and at a cosmic geographic location conducive to its proper use, remained in service until 1521, when the conquistadors ordered the systematic destruction of everything in Tenochtitlán, to the point that no stone might stand atop any other stone: an exhaustive demolition of houses, temples, palaces, monoliths, pyramids, as well as a vast library of codices, a repository of the accumulated Mayan wisdom of the ages.

In 1790, what remained of the stone was salvaged and studied. Of the 500 years that this stone, or Aztec Calendar, has existed, it spent approximately 269 of them buried, thus surviving many vicissitudes. For this reason some call it the Piedra Milagro, "miraculous stone," since it was not destroyed like so many others. Like the Coyolxauhqui, it remained buried, unknown to the conquistadors and the warriors who accompanied them and who took pleasure in demolishing this great metropolis stone by stone. How is it possible that they never saw it?

Only the renowned Mexican astronomer and archeologist Don Antonio de León y Gama (1735–1802) was privy to the first initiation into the stone's secrets; he worked closely with it, comparing the information on it to the Christian calendar and recording his knowledge faithfully. What he left to us was his work comparing the calendar on the stone with the Christian calendar, with the Nahua numbers of the hieroglyphs. This includes the geometric and chronological use of the eight points (*ahujeros*) where lines are drawn for finding the solstices and equinoxes, as well as the elements for using the stone as a sundial. More importantly, Don Antonio was the first to give this stone the name by which it is now known to the entire world: the Aztec Calendar.

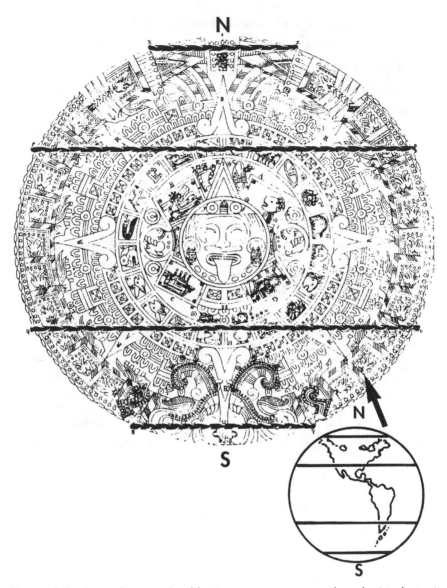

Figure 3.2. According to the Mexican astronomer-archaeologist Antonio de León y Gama, the Nahua, or Aztecs, placed certain lines on the Tonal Machiotl, or Stone of the Sun, to indicate the movements of the Sun. The smaller drawing here shows some of the markings, or imaginary lines, transferred to Earth, indicating the movements of the Sun. This aids in the understanding of the solstices and equinoxes. Comparing these two drawings, we may note the great similarity in their appearance and use; the difference is that one represents the microcosm, and the other represents the macrocosm of the world.

Why was it officially named Cuauhxicalli? Why was it then known as the Aztec Calendar? What was its true, original name, and where should it be placed in order to use it most effectively?

A replica of the monument should be made and placed in the open air, under glass, in the exact location in the *zócalo* (main plaza) that was its original position, so that it may be known, admired, and used by all the visitors who come to this metropolis—and also to do justice to a monument that was the synthesis of the scientific knowledge of the Mesoamerican peoples, and which preserves the applications in its spiral chronology that are still relevant to our daily lives. But it should officially be given its Nahuatl name to describe it correctly: combining the words *tonal,* "suns," and *machiotl,* "diagram," to comprise the name Tonal Machiotl—"The Diagram of the Suns that Have Been and Will Be."

Calendrical Pyramids: Kukulcán, Niches of El Tajín, and Quetzalcoatl

At the Temple of Kukulcán, the Temple of the Niches of El Tajín, the Temple of Quetzalcoatl, and other pyramids throughout Mesoamerica, the wisdom humankind needs at this time can be viscerally experienced and directly accessed. These sacred sites have the ability to raise a person's consciousness level by virtue of the fact that such sites vibrate to a higher-dimensional frequency. These sacred sites are the legacy of humanity, and it is our duty to search them out, like the Maya of old, for the profound initiatory knowledge they contain that will lead us to understanding the reality of this third dimension in which we exist. When you visit such sites, you open your nervous system to receive the information that has been stored there. A pyramid thus acts as your teacher, helping to prepare your consciousness to receive higher vibrations.

Kukulcán

The pyramids of Mesoamerica are essentially giant astronomical computers representing the sacred geometry on which the Mayan calendars are based. The marvelous pyramidal structure at Chichén Itzá called the Temple of Kukulcán, in the Yucatán, was built at least 2,500 years ago. Every year, at the time of the spring and fall equinoxes, tens of thousands of people come to visit this sacred site, which is a technology that still works just as it did when the Maya first built it.

For the Mayan people, the magical appearance of Kukulcán on the side of the pyramid is a significant cultural event. This occurs when, as the Sun rises higher and higher around March 21 and September 21 of each year, the steps on one side of the pyramid create triangle shadows that connect, one at a time, from the top of the pyramid to the base of the pyramid. At the base of the steps is the carved head of a serpent. Once the seventh triangle is connected, at about five o'clock in the afternoon of the equinox, the head of the serpent then connects to the seven triangles of shadow that create the length of its tail extending to the top of the pyramid (see figure 3.3c), and the magical spirit of this pyramid calendar can be experienced firsthand. At the exact moment that this occurs, there is a great celebration by the thousands of people who have come to witness this phenomenon. You feel a jolt of electric energy from the base of your spine all the way up as you experience the cosmic serpent of light that has descended from the heavens and joined with your own body.

This event reveals the Mayan sages' profound understanding of the connection between mathematics and the cosmos. They knew that the spring equinox occurs when the Sun, at the center position, or equator, of Earth, passes from the southern hemisphere to the northern hemisphere (or vice versa). The Maya not only incorporated this date into their pyramids, but they also incorporated the rotation and passage of such planets as Mars, Jupiter, Venus, and so forth, making it a true cosmic calendar-clock of masterful construction.

The calendrical information in the Pyramid of Kukulcán can be

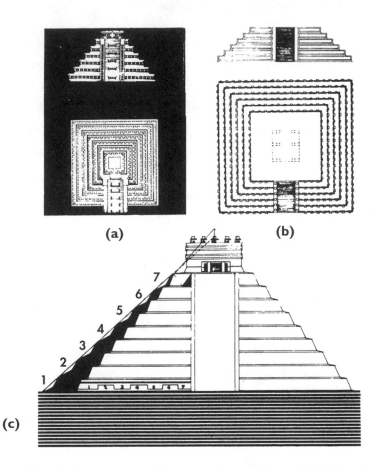

(a) (b)

(c)

Figure 3.3. (a) The pyramidal Temple of the Niches of El Tajín, Veracruz. The niches of this first Mesoamerican pyramid are cosmic calendar markers. It is still not precisely known which people built this pyramid, nor is its original name known. Our true indigenous culture is carved into the stones of these ancient temples. (b) The pyramidal Temple of Quetzalcoatl, Mexico State. The gods emerged at this place; the sages and masters lived at this temple for many thousands of years, worshipping Father Sun and Mother Earth. Knowing the profound meaning of Quetzalcoatl—one who has fully developed all the faculties of consciousness—comes through the mastery of religion, philosophy, mathematics, astronomy, and the other sciences of the ancient peoples of Mesoamerica. (c) Temple of Kukulcán, Yucatán, the temple of the seven triangles. The vast majority of humankind is unaware of its symbolism. Every year at the spring and fall equinoxes, in the evening, one can see these seven triangles marking the equinoxes, the time when we say that the Sun is at the center of Earth, also known as the equator. Viewed another way—from the esoteric viewpoint, we might say—these seven triangles are related to the seven chakras.

found in its ninety-one steps that mark the four seasons (see figure 3.4). Because the pyramid has four sides, $4 \times 91 = 364$, it makes a total of 364 intervals, or days. Each side of the pyramid is thus an indicator of each season of the year, making 91 days of spring, 91 days of summer, 91 days of autumn, and 91 days of winter. The Pyramid of Kukulcán incorporates other Mayan calendars, including the Tun Uc, Haab, Tzolk'in, and Tunben K'ak', which will be discussed at greater length in chapters 6 and 7, and probably other calendars that have since been lost to us, and is in itself an example of the synchronization of all the Mayan calendars.

Niches of El Tajín

The pyramidal Temple of the Niches of El Tajín, in Veracruz, Mexico, was built by an unknown people. In this sacred city of El Tajín, Huracán, the god of fierce winds, was worshipped. This millenarian sacred temple is an important religious site that survived one of the last great deluges, some 12,000 years ago—a monument of exquisite proportions, built with the application of deep knowledge, in which calendars can be found engraved in the architecture (see figure 3.3a). It is important to point out certain aspects of its architecture, because there is nothing similar to it in all of Mesoamerica.

This pyramid's niches contain Mesoamerican wisdom related to the calendars. On the main staircase, one can see four groups of three niches, resembling altars, plus a central one above, making a total of thirteen niches, and resulting in the equation $4 \times 3 = 12 + 1 = 13$ (the significance of the number 13 to the Maya will be discussed in the next chapter). The pyramid is made up of six levels, the first having two niches; the second, four; the third, eight; the fourth, ten; the fifth, twelve; and the sixth, sixteen. The front part of this pyramid has a total of fifty-two niches, a number that corresponds to the Tunben K'ak' ("New Fire" or Pleiadian) calendar of 52 years (which will be discussed in greater detail later in this book). If we add the number 13 to this quantity, the result is $52 + 13 = 65$. This new number is a quarter of the 260-day sacred Tzolk'in calendar of the Maya.

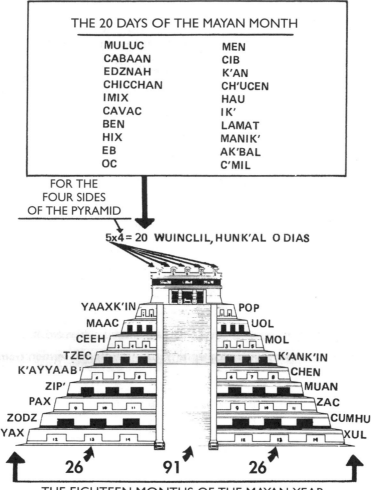

Figure 3.4. This image shows the Pyramid of Kukulcán, in Chichén Itzá, Yucatán, Mexico. In the rectangular part at the top, the 20 days of the Mayan month in the Haab, the solar calendar, are indicated; the upper part of the pyramid expresses the manner in which the Maya kept track of the days and months. Moreover, on the sides of the pyramid one can see the 18 months of the Mayan year, and in the lower part the 26 marks on the left and right sides; in the center, the pyramid has 91 steps, or levels, corresponding to the seasons. It was surely in this place that the Maya developed many of their calendars; in fact, here is an illustration of this point:

18 x 20 = 360 days in the Haab calendar.
26 + 26 = 52 years in the Tunben K'ak' calendar.
91 x 4 = 364 days in the lunar Tun Uc calendar.

Quetzalcoatl

At the sacred pyramidal Temple of Quetzalcoatl, Father Sun was worshipped as the bearer of life (see figure 3.3b). As I noted in my book *Secrets of Mayan Science/Religion,* the secret, or inner, meaning of Quetzalcoatl (Kukulcán in the Mayan language) is one who not only knows the seven psychospiritual forces that govern our bodies but who also uses them and understands their intimate relationship with natural and cosmic laws. In Mesoamerica, such masters existed, which is why this temple, located in Teotihuacán, Mexico State, was so revered. The translation of the word *Teotihuacán* demonstrates the presence of the Mayan influence in this sacred site: *teo,* meaning "god"; *ti,* "place"; *hua,* "emerge"; and *can,* "wisdom." Thus the translation of the name is "The Place Where God's Wisdom Emerges." Over a period of many centuries, innumerable ceremonies took place here.

Like the other pyramids, the Temple of Quetzalcoatl offers knowledge of the calendars engraved in its pyramidal shape. On the main part we can discern sixty-six markings, plus twelve others on the sides of the steps. On the side that faces south there are ninety-six markings; there are another ninety-six on the side that faces east; and another ninety-six on the side that faces north. And so 66 + 12 + 96 + 96 + 96 = 366—a figure that may represent days, years, or intervals.

Astronomical Observatory of Chichén Itzá

In modern times, many advances have been made in the science of astronomy, and many nations have great astronomical centers, from which celestial bodies at great distances are observed. Unfortunately, this science, for the most part, is not accessible to the general public, for which reason most of humanity is ignorant not only of astronomy, but of their cosmic spiritual heritage.

In the days of the ancient Maya, however, even ordinary people were far better educated in understanding the nature of the cosmos, because the science of astronomy, like their calendars, was woven into the fabric of their everyday lives. The Maya considered astronomy to be intertwined with astrology, rather than being separate from it, as it is often regarded today. Thus these two sciences together aided the Maya and were part of their politics, religion, agriculture, calendars, architecture, rituals—indeed, the entire social order of this civilization. This is demonstrated in their manuscripts, or codices; in their stone inscriptions, which can be seen at all their ceremonial centers; and in the construction of the temples themselves, a process in which architectural features related to certain celestial phenomena that were important for calendrical reasons, as we have noted previously in this chapter.

The ancient Itzae built the astronomical observatory seen in figure 3.5 (which is known today by its Spanish name, El Caracol, "The Snail," because it has a staircase that winds like a snail's shell), in Chichén Itzá, a center of Mayan learning. The ancients possessed a practical technology for observing the cosmos, with apparatuses that were simple and functional. The base of this temple was built with various square levels; the upper part was built in the form of a circle, in order to be able to observe the cosmos with greater ease. The upper part may be viewed as half a sphere, with a few small windows that served as observatories for watching planets and other bodies of the cosmos and for observing solstices and equinoxes, the times when our Father Sun ascends and descends in all his cosmic magnitude, with all the movement of which the Creator of life is capable. At night, one can see the sky full of stars, just as the Mayan astronomers saw it, observing such celestial bodies as Yaax Ek' (Jupiter); Chac Ek' (Mars); Xux Ek' (Mercury); Ain Ek' (Saturn); Zac Ek' (Venus); K'in, (our Sun); Xaman Ek' (the Pole Star). As we noted earlier, the names of the Moon in the Mayan language are U, Uh, and Uc—words that are represented by the number 7. Thus the Maya connected it with the Pleiades, a subject we will further explore in the next chapter.

The Chilam Balam, in this case the priest or sacred prophet, and the Hauk'in, the master teacher, were responsible for this scientific place. All that they observed was used in the centers of learning in order to educate the public; thus the Mayan people learned the secrets that the scientists were discovering, secrets that were then recorded in writing in the Mayan codices and the chronicles of the history of humanity that were read to the public on special occasions. Moreover, the equinoxes and solstices of each year were observed by the Chilam Balam and all the people gathered in the ceremonial center, which calls to mind the great rituals the Maya performed when the planets brought about certain phenomena such as an eclipse. How magnificent it would have been, dear reader, to have taken part in those rituals with the great Mayan seers of these temples!

The magnificent architecture of this temple from which the Itzae observed the celestial dome can be seen in figure 3.5. In our solar system,

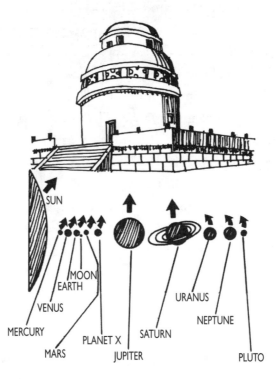

Figure 3.5. Astronomical observatory of Chichén Itzá, Yucatán, Mexico. This observatory is the place where the Chilam Balam and the Hauk'in watched the heavenly bodies and recorded their movements mathematically in their codices. They also used this information to formulate their astronomical calendars.

North

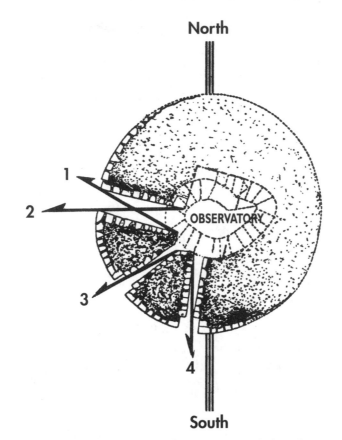

South

Figure 3.6. Horizontal cross-section of the cupola of the observatory at Chichén Itzá, Yucatán, also known as El Caracol (drawing according to Sylvanus Morley):
1. Indicates the position of the Moon at its greatest northern declination, coinciding with March 21.
2. Western sunset point, coinciding with March 21 each year: the spring equinox.
3. Indicates the position of the Moon at its maximum southern declination, coinciding with December 21.
4. Geographic south.

there is a belt of asteroids that according to scientists are the remains of a planet that exploded, known today as Planet X, or Nibiru, as seen in the drawing. As was reported by the scholar Hugh Harleston Jr., it is well known that ancient peoples such as the Teotihuacanos recorded this planet in their sacred city of Teotihuacán.

The Great Idol of Tiwanak'u, Bolivia

Forms of Mesoamerican calendars can be found throughout the Americas. One example is the so-called Great Idol of Tiwanak'u. In reality a monolith representing a priest of Pachamama (literally, "Earth Mother"), it has been referred to by Eurocentric archaeologists as the Bennett Monolith, after Wendell Bennett, the archaeologist who unearthed it in 1932, where it had been buried in the complex of ruins on the Bolivian altiplano called Tiwanak'u. This monolith measures 7.30 meters in length by 1.30 meters in width and is intricately carved with the same iconography found at the Gateway of the Sun, at the same site, including the same calendar inscriptions. It is necessary to study this statue carefully, as did the Austrian naval engineer, geomorphologist, and naturalized Bolivian Arthur Posnansky, who visited the ancient site while it was being excavated and became so mesmerized that he later dubbed himself the Apostle of Tiwanak'u. He later wrote about how he dragged himself in the mud to lie underneath the monolith, then being excavated, and, candle in hand, removed the mud off the back of the statue with his fingernails, marveling at the intricate carvings thus exposed. Posnansky was responsible for removing the statue from Tiwank'u to the Bolivian capital of La Paz. It was returned to the native Aymara people at Tiwanak'u in 2002.

Posnansky wrote, "The idol of Tiwanak'u holds what appears to be a vessel (*keru*) in its left hand, which may be a *clepsidra* (hourglass). In his belt appear a series of lobsters, which are possibly equivalent to crayfish, namely, the zodiacal sign of the Age of Cancer" (see figure 3.7).

Let us analyze Posnansky's last comparison. Taking European astrology, with its origins in Greek mythology, into consideration, we might mention that the ancient Greeks drew their astrological and astronomical knowledge, along with a great deal of their culture, from the Egyptians. For example, if we examine the form of the Great Sphinx of Egypt, we will see that its body resembles that of the lion (Leo). For this reason, we can infer that the figure of the crayfish in

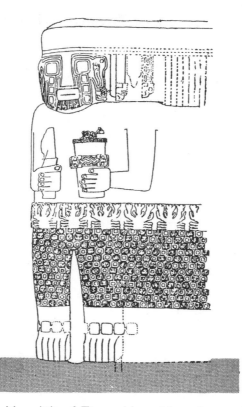

Figure 3.7. The Monolith of Tiwanak'u, with various calendrical symbols depicted on the figure (drawing from Posnansky).

the belt of the monolith of Tiwanak'u represents the sign of Cancer.

Returning to the present time, we have now passed through the astrological epochs of Leo, Cancer, Gemini, Taurus, Aries, and Pisces, to finally arrive at Aquarius. Each of these cycles, or ages, according to the Greek-Egyptian-based European astrology, is equivalent to approximately 2,000 years. The sum of 2,000 × 6 = 12,000 years, plus 55 years is 12,055 years.

Dick Edgar Ibarra Grasso, in his book *Ciencia en Tiwanak'u en el Incaico,* says: "In the idol's face and hair, the only important details that we must consider are the braids, at intervals, which form a set of 20." Remember that this number 20, the number of measure (which we will discuss in more detail in the next chapter), is a number found in all the Mesoamerican calendars, from Alaska to Patagonia—which is to say from the North Pole to the South Pole.

Other symbols may be observed on this Tiwanak'u monolith, for instance, its skirt, which displays 182 double circles. If we consider the total sum of circles in the 182 double circles, 182 + 182 = 364, we obtain the number 364, which represents days, or intervals. According to Posnansky, the Aymara people who lived in Bolivia and who built this ceremonial center used the lunar calendar. If we multiply 13 (the number of lunar cycles in a year) by 28 (the length of a lunar cycle), we get 364. This measure is the same one used by the Tiwanakotas, or Aymara: 182 + 182 = 364 days, or intervals. Posnansky says the Aymara who built this ceremonial center were the most ancient people who inhabited the earth, more ancient than the Inca of Peru, who also used the same calendar, as well as others.

4

COSMIC INDICATORS
OF THE MAYA

Through their astronomical observations, their religious beliefs, and their philosophy, the Maya concluded that Hunab K'u transmits radiant energy through the stars. As noted by José Argüelles in his book *The Mayan Factor,* these stars in turn serve as lenses in transmitting this energy to planets. In our planetary system, the Sun is the chief mediator of Hunab K'u—the lens by which Earth directly receives cosmic information. The Maya perceived the pulsations or vibrations of Hunab K'u in a language of sacred numbers, and they developed complex mathematical frameworks through which astronomical and calendrical cycles could be viewed as interconnected parts of a grand astronomical order. This incredible knowledge of cosmic law was the legacy of thousands of years of Mayan civilization.

Dualism and the Mayan Cosmic Order

An important principle in Mesoamerican thought is dualism. All the indigenous cultures of Mesoamerica were eminently dualistic, meaning that they perceived everything in terms of pairs, similar to the Taoist principle of yin and yang, light and dark, active and passive—referring to the complementary, interdependent dualism of reciprocal interaction that occurs throughout nature. This principle of dualism in which the Maya saw all of life also encompassed the mathematics of their calendars. Therefore, when the Maya conceived of the universe surrounding us, they viewed it as being dual. For example, their concept of God, Hunab K'u, was represented by a circle and a square, a prime example of duality represented geometrically. When they referred to Hunab K'u, they called him the Bearer of Movement and Measure, which again reflects the aspect of duality.

And so without delving any further into this profound subject with deep philosophical implications, the reader should remember that as we progress in this discussion of the Mayan astronomical calendars, understanding the fact that the Mayan world was conceived in terms of duality is fundamental to comprehending how the number system in the Mayan astronomical calendars works.

Significance of the Number 13

Figure 4.1 shows a Mayan tablet analyzed by anthropologist Pierre Ivanoff in his book *En el país de los Mayas*. This tablet, found in the Dos Pilas archaeological zone in Guatemala, was decoded specifically for its numerological, mathematical, and calendar aspects. It also contains further details of Mayan culture that may well be deciphered at some future time.

In his book, Ivanoff poses questions regarding the true meaning of the number 13. Allow me to give a brief explanation of the way in which the ancient Maya used this sacred number, and of the manner in which it is necessary to understand it in order to comprehend the Mayan culture. One must first differentiate between symbology, the art of expression by symbols, and numerology, the study of the occult significance of numbers. Recall that in chapter 2 we understood Hunab K'u to be the Giver of Movement and Measure. In Mayan culture, the circle has the symbolic value of 13, representing both movement and spirit. This number also represents the 13 great articulations of the human being, the 13 planets of our solar system, the 13 cycles of the Moon, and so forth.

In other words, the Maya clearly understood that all of creation is

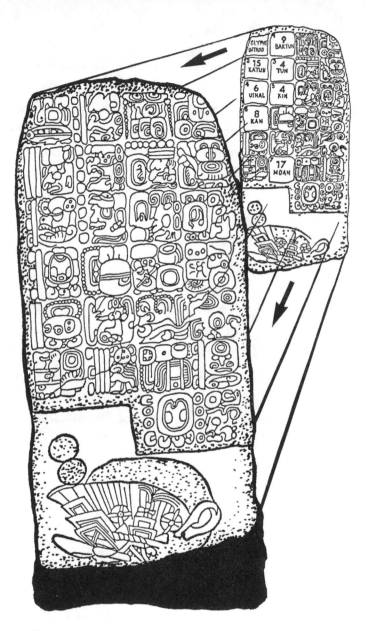

Figure 4.1. This tablet was found in the archaeological zone of Dos Pilas, Estela 2, in Guatemala. As one can see, it has only been possible to translate the numerological aspects of this carving.

9	Baktun	9 × 144,000	=	1,296,000 days
15	Katun	15 × 7,200	=	108,000 days
4	Tun	4 × 360	=	1,440 days
6	Uinal	6 × 20	=	120 days
4	Kin	4 × 1	=	4 days
			Total:	1,405,564 days

divided by the number 13. The Mayan priests had a system of timekeeping for each day, in which it was equally divided into 13 sections, or intervals, that we would call hours. Each section was further divided into 13 segments that we would call minutes, which were further divided by 13 to create what we call seconds. Each second was further divided by 13, and divided again and again, to infinity. So each and every moment experienced by the Maya was divided infinitely by the number 13. This process also expanded infinitely in the other direction—into the macrocosm of the whole universe.

And so this number 13 is the key to understanding how the Mayan calendars work together, or synchronize, to express cosmic laws. The Maya had 13 constellations in their zodiac—they included the Pleiades; the day and night each had 13 intervals (in contrast to the 24 hours used today to measure the day and night together, which does not relate to any natural cycle). In the equation $13 \times 4 = 52$, we mark the cycle of 52 years that formed the Tunben K'ak', or Calendar of the New Fire (see chapter 6), which marks a full cycle of the Pleiades. In the equation $13 \times 20 = 260$ (recall that 20 is the number that represents measure, represented by the square, with Hunab K'u communicated as the *union* of 20 and 13), we have the Tzolk'in calendar—260 days or 260 intervals: this is the calendar used for making astrological charts and is also called the sacred, or divinatory, calendar.

13:20—The Universal Timing Frequency

As we know, the modern world divides the day and night into twelve hours each, and the year into twelve months. Hence the number 12 is the key to the modern world's view of time. However, this is an artificial timing because these cycles do not synchronize with any natural cycle on Earth or in the cosmos. So while the Gregorian calendar system has 12 months, and this roughly approximates the length of a solar year, the months are irregular and do not synchronize with anything in nature. Furthermore, the artificial units called "seconds" and "minutes" do not relate to anything in the natural world, either.

As a result of this false timing of the modern world, human beings are alienated from synchronizing with the natural world and with the present moment—and it is only in the present moment that the human being can realize that the self is infinitely interconnected with everything else that exists, has existed, and will exist. And so the Gregorian calendar system has led to a severe case of amnesia, in which human beings have forgotten that we are each of us cosmic beings, eternally connected to the one source of all that is: Hunab K'u.

The Maya, on the other hand, used the natural timing frequencies that are based on the number 13, the number of movement, and the number 20, the number of measure. We have just discussed the significance of the number 13, but why is 20 the number of measure? The Mayan counting system, as we know, is done by 20s, not 10s, as in the decimal system. On the simplest level, the number 20 signifies the number of digits a person has—ten fingers and ten toes. Archaeologists and others who have studied the Mayan system acknowledge that counting in 20s allows for a very rapid summing up of large numbers. Why the Maya were contemplating such large numbers remains a mystery to them.

Contemplating the real significance of the number 20 is somewhat of an intuitive process. Its true significance lies in its *relationship* to the number 13. This 13:20 ratio is not a Mayan invention. It was discovered by José Argüelles on December 10, 1989, as described in *Time and the Technosphere*. As Argüelles explains, the 13:20 ratio is a universal timing frequency that synchronizes the whole of creation, from the infinitesimally small to the infinitely large—meaning that it is a general pattern that creation naturally follows. It is the proportion in which your human body is laid out (for example, thirteen major joints in the human body and twenty digits, as we just noted), the proportion of land mass to water on this Planet Earth, and so forth, echoing throughout creation. It is also the ratio that forms the basis of all sacred geometry, such as in the pyramids that we discussed in the last chapter.

And so this natural timing of 13:20 is a cosmic indicator based on relationships inherent in natural processes: on the macrocosmic level, in the motion of the stars, planets, and galaxies; on the microcosmic level, as reflected in the proportions of the human body and the biological rhythms of plants and animals; and even further still, on the infinite level, in the subtle inner-dimensional movements of consciousness and mind. It is like the processes of division and multiplication: we find that it is consciousness that divides creation, by a factor of 13, because it is only when we are conscious of something that we can appreciate that part of creation; and it is creation that multiplies, by a factor of 20, the number of measure.

As Above, So Below

A collection of the symbolic, ideographic, and iconographic knowledge of cosmic laws, handed down through the ages, the Chilam Balam of Chumayel connects us with our ancestors' lineage. The Mayan priests, knowing with their foresight that an era of Mayan tradition was coming to a close with the coming of a new religion, saw the need to record all they knew about the great Mayan civilization in this sacred book. From this particular chronicle we can learn how the Maya used mathematics, astronomy, astrology, religion, and philosophy in their calendars. This and other evidence will serve to refute the mainstream scholars, who claim that when the Spaniards arrived on the Yucatán the Mayan culture had already vanished into history.

The Maya were not the only people with knowledge of cosmic laws; other ancients, including the peoples of Mesoamerica as well as the Babylonians, Sumerians, and Egyptians, also had scientific knowledge of cosmic laws, and they, too, recorded their knowledge in their various codices. What the Chilam Balam of Chumayel reveals, as seen in the drawing in figure 4.2(a), is what the European scientists during the scientific revolution had been struggling to find, beginning with the German mathematician, astronomer, and astrologer Johannes Kepler (1571–1630). Kepler wanted to gain knowledge of the cosmos, its mathematics, and made many interesting scientific discoveries along the way. However, he made a big error when he omitted the human being in his calculations.

The drawing that appears in figure 4.2(a), based on one from the Chilam Balam of Chumayel, delineates 13 intervals, or movements of the Sun, and tells us that the human being must be included in the cosmic laws, with the body in contact with Earth and the head represented as the Sun, or solar center. In other words, the human being is a microcosm of the universe, and is therefore inseparable from cosmic law. The center, or halfway point, of the number 13 is the number 7. This codex also tells us that the human body has the number 7 in its feet and the number 13 in part of its neck. Figure 4.2(b) is a more artistic interpretation of the same drawing, which besides the 13 numbers includes the

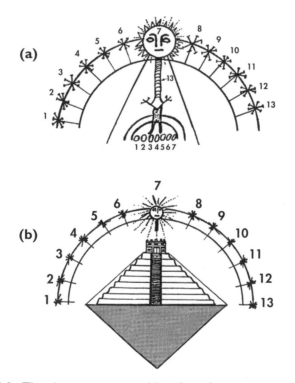

Figure 4.2. The drawing on top (a) is based on an image from the Chilam Balam of Chumayel and offers us an important teaching from the Mayan civilization about cosmic law. The original drawing showed several marks in the form of a semicircle; after a great deal of study and meditation, it was possible to decipher it as shown here. In the upper part is the Sun, connected to the human body; here the Mayan priests are telling us that the human being is part of the Sun. The pyramid, in the drawing below (b), is also shown in union with the Sun and the human being.

Pyramid of Kukulcán, in Chichén Itzá; this serves to give an even better idea of the cosmic vision of the Maya.

Figure 4.2(b), inspired by the first drawing, is our interpretation of what the Maya were telling us. This drawing also shows the 13 marks, or intervals, on the semicircular part; as we know, the midpoint of 13 is 7, and this number is inside the Sun. This drawing confirms that the day has 13 intervals, or Mayan hours; logically, the night must also have 13 intervals, or hours. These two quantities give us a total of 26 intervals, or hours. In the lower part of figure 4.2(a) we find 7 marks with circles. This number 7 is indicative of many things: recall, as one example, from chapter 3, the seven triangles formed on the Pyramid of Kukulcán, in Chichén Itzá, every year during the equinoxes.

Significance of the Number 7

The group of stars known as the Pleiades, or Seven Sisters, called Tzek'eb by the Maya, was represented by the seven rattles of the serpent (recall our discussion in the previous chapter of the significance of the serpent appearing on the Pyramid of Kukulcán). As we noted in chapter 1, these seven stars were central to the ancient Maya, because according to their beliefs life began on Planet Earth at the same time this star group first settled in its place in the sky, and human consciousness has its origins there.

Let us refer to the Pyramid of Kukulcán to examine the relationship between this calendrical monument and the Pleiades. Fifty-two great marks can be seen on each of the four sides of this pyramid. This number, 52, is related to the Tunben K'ak', or Pleiadian calendar. The indigenous peoples of the Americas celebrated the complete cycle of this calendar every 52 years in a New Fire ceremony, a ceremony of renewal to mark the initiating point of the new calendar round corresponding to the complete lesser cycle of the Tzek'eb.

As noted in the previous chapter, every year on the spring and fall equinoxes, as the Sun begins to set, seven marks can be seen on the steps of the Pyramid of Kukulcán. These seven triangles, produced by the play of shadow and light, tell us a great many things about the Mayan culture. Let us pay heed to what the scholar Rodolfo Benavides tells us in his book *Dramáticas profecías de la Gran Pirámide* (Dramatic Prophecies of the Great Pyramid) regarding the stars of the Tzek'eb:

> The astronomer José Comas Sola devoted a particular effort to studying this group of stars, and after many years of direct observation and photographing he came to the conclusion that at least six more visible stars—seven if Alcyone is included—form a true physical system; in other words, these stars do not live and move independently; rather, they obey a gravitational center, revolving much as the planets do around [our] Sun.
>
> Various famous astronomers have performed studies and minute calculations concerning the same subject and have arrived at the conclusion that the Pleiades are, in effect, a system of suns that revolve around Alcyone. Oriental astrophysics, for its part, recognizes Alcyone as the center of the solar orbit. Likewise, the balance of the terrestrial axis, which produces a series of phenomena, among them the procession of the equinoxes, is probably very closely related to Alcyone. . . . Generally speaking, we have examined what astronomy tells us; now, speculating on our own, we may suppose that each of these suns is the center of its own planetary system, and, naturally, that each of these planets may be a world with its own vegetable, animal, and human life.
>
> In the [1949] book *Der Jüngste Tag* [The Recent Day], by the German writer Paul Otto Hesse, tantalizing statements appear regarding the Pleiades. Hesse says that our planetary system forms part of the system of suns belonging to the system of the Pleiades—which is to say that there are not six suns revolving around Alcyone, but instead many more, and that our own Sun occupies the seventh orbit, which revolves in a space of 24,000 years, divided into two periods of 12,000 years each, 2,000 of which are years of "light" and 10,000 years of "darkness." According to Hesse, we are now living at

the end of 10,000 years of darkness, and consequently we are about to enter 2,000 years of light.

Let us analyze what is being said here. Since the very beginning, the Maya have claimed that the Pleiades is the axis of life on Earth; they consistently included this constellation in their various calendars. They also included the number 7 in their culture and in their calendars in a pervasive and profound manner. I will attempt to give a simple explanation of how the Mayan people used this number 7, and in what manner they included it in their culture.

The Pleiades are composed of seven principal stars, or suns; the Maya deduced that each of these suns deposited its energetic power in us when we human beings were formed, meaning that we in fact possess the power of these suns—we each have these seven powers of our solar family within our own individual bodies. It should also be understood that all manifestations of life on Earth include this number 7 as part of its energy. If this number is present in all that has physical form, then it must also be present in all that is invisible, or has no discernable physical form (recall our earlier discussion about dualism in Mayan thought). Consequently, in our initiatory process of study and comprehension, we are obliged to penetrate the true meaning of the number 7, on both the physical and spiritual levels.

Thus, for the ancient Maya, the Pleiades represented the principle of life on Planet Earth, and this is why it formed their cultural axis. Mayan religion and mathematics were intimately connected with the seven stars, or suns, of the Pleiades, and as a result, all the Mayan astronomical calendars were also connected to the Pleiades. The Maya performed great rituals at the time of the equinoxes, when the seven isosceles triangles appeared on the Pyramid of Kukulcán, in Chichén Itzá. But the most important rituals were celebrated every 52 years, according to the Tunben K'ak' calendar, which marks one of the lesser cycles of the Pleiades. Of the many calendars of the ancient Maya, behind them all was the calendar of the great cycle of 26,000 years—the time it takes

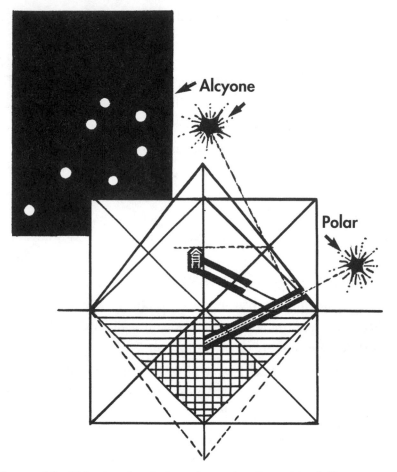

Figure 4.3. This drawing is based on the Pyramid of Cheops, in Egypt. Alcyone is the center of the Pleiades; in the Mayan language the Pleiades are called Tzek'eb. "Polar" indicates the Pole Star. The Egyptians, along with other ancient peoples, including the Maya, the Babylonians, the Inca, the Aymara, the Cherokee, and the Aztecs, all knew about the system of suns known as the Pleiades.

for our Sun to complete a single revolution around Alcyone, the central star of the Pleiades, with all our galaxy's orbiting planets accompanying it. The calendar that marks this great cycle, like the star group itself, was called Tzek'eb in the Mayan language.

5

MAYAN
UNITS OF TIME

We have discussed how, from the perspective of the Maya, there is one source of all energy: divine consciousness, or Hunab K'u, which manifests as an infinite number of possible forms throughout all dimensions. This Hunab K'u is the heart of all beings, and each of us is connected through our hearts. In fact, it is impossible to be disconnected!

The Maya considered each of the infinite forms of Hunab K'u to consist of frequency vibrations or tonalities; in fact, they regarded all matter as being interconnected waves of energy, or vibration. So unlike the modern world, which is obsessed with material reality and linear time, the Maya based their understanding of reality on frequencies and vibrations—the unseen as well as the seen. And so as we move further into this discussion of the Mayan calendars and the numbers that are intrinsic to them, it will be helpful to remember that we are talking about harmonic resonances, the modern term given by José Argüelles to describe this phenomenon. Numbers, within the Mayan system of thought, are not specifically and only related to physical quantities; all numbers, including zero, represent unique frequencies and tones.

Recall that in chapter 3 we mentioned Fray Diego de Landa, the Spaniard who was responsible for destroying most of the Mayan civilization's vast library of codices containing their cosmic knowledge. When this Franciscan friar first arrived in the land of the Maya, he made it his mission to walk the length and breadth of the Yucatán. He was willing to go into lands where the native peoples deeply resented the Spanish, armed with nothing more than sheer determination to learn everything he could about Mayan culture, including their writing and numeric system—so that it would be easy for him to destroy it in the future. As a result, he became one of the first European "experts" to make compilations of the Mayan culture and its calendars.

Unfortunately, this Spanish friar did not comprehend anything about what he observed in the calendars, or in any of the other sacred writings the Mayan native people showed him for that matter, due to the fundamental misconception that men like him had inherited from the European system of keeping time. Consequently, Fray Landa was disoriented, and his subsequent writings concerning the Mayan culture are fundamentally wrong. Yet Landa's inaccurate and even fanciful "history" became the prism through which most of the European world has since learned about the Maya, continuing his legacy of untruths.

We will now examine one example of what Landa wrote, concerning the chronology of the calendars, especially the Haab, or solar calendar of the Maya, taken from his book *Relación de las cosas de Yucatán y sus Indios*:

> In either of the months of *Pop* or *Cumhu,* on the day indicated by the priest, they held a festival that they called *Ocn (Ocnah)*, which means "Renewal of the Temple." This festival was held in honor of the Chacs, who they held to be the gods of the maize fields, and at the festival they received the predictions of the Bacabes. This festival took place year after year, and this was also the time for renewing their earthenware idols and their incense burners. It was customary for each idol to have an incense burner for producing fragrance, and if necessary, the house was rebuilt or renovated, and on the walls hieroglyphs were written, recording the memory of these things.

All this serves only to confirm one notable fact: that precisely between the months of December and March, the Maya performed these rituals and ceremonies to mark the end of the old year and the beginning of the new. Thus according to Fray Landa, only one thing is certain: the Maya used the Haab—but they used other calendars as well—to track the record of solstices and equinoxes, in order to know the movements of the Sun.

The 13 Divisions of Day and of Night

Figure 5.1 (see page 73) will henceforth serve as our pattern for connecting the Mayan mathematical keys and understanding the Mayan astronomical calendars, and we will be referring back to it periodically. The basic unit of time in the Mayan calendar is called a *k'in*. This word means "day," "sun," "person," or "relative"; the Maya tracked their cycles one k'in at a time. The word *ak'ab,* as seen in the Mayan night divisions, means "night." As we know, the Maya divided the day and night into 13 intervals, or hours, each, making a total of 26 intervals, or hours. Here are the Mayan names of these intervals, and their English-language translations. Note the similarity in the patterns of naming the divisions of day and night.

Mayan Day Divisions

1. K'in   day
2. Bul k'in   the whole day
3. Tip'il k'in   sunrise
4. Chun k'in   from 7 a.m. to 11 a.m.
5. Chumuc k'in   high noon
6. Hun zut k'in   a moment in the day
7. Xot k'in   a fraction of the day
8. Pot k'in   divider of the day
9. Zazil k'in   the brightening of the day
10. Ich k'in   the eye of day
11. Chinil k'in   the evening
12. Ocnah k'in   sunset
13. Hatz k'in   darkness

Mayan Night Divisions

1. Ak'ab   night
2. Bul ak'ab   the whole night
3. Tip'il ak'ab   beginning of the night
4. Chun ak'ab   from 7 p.m. to 11 p.m.
5. Chumac ak'ab   midnight
6. Hun zut ak'ab   a moment in the night
7. Xot ak'ab   a fraction of the night
8. Pot ak'ab   divider of the night
9. Zzazil ak'ab   the brightening of the night
10. Ich ak'ab   eye of the night
11. Chinil ak'ab   the dawn
12. Ocnah ak'ab   the end of the night
13. Hatz ak'ab   light

The 18 Months of the Haab Calendar

The Spanish friar Landa's erroneous transcriptions of the Mayan words for the 18 months (consisting of 20 days per month) of the Haab calendar will not be shown here; suffice it to say that the Mayan priests of the Yucatán distrusted the Spanish invaders right from the start, this persistent friar no less. For this reason, they never would have told Landa the whole truth about the Mayan culture; they kept their sacred treasures—and numbers and their meanings were indeed considered sacred—hidden from these ignorant barbarians. And so the hieroglyphs that Landa duplicated in his book are not even useful for understanding the true Mayan culture.

The following are the true names and meanings of the 18 months of the Mayan Haab. Note that there are 18 months plus another short month or interval of 5 days called Uayeb.

1. Pop   leader, chief, counselor, ruler
2. Uo   understanding, patience, talent, serenity
3. Zip   maturity, usefulness, plenitude, availability

   4. Zodz   intuition, vision, clairvoyance, perception

   5. Tzeek   inventiveness, curiosity, perseverance, quest

   6. Xul   goal, purpose, end, cycle

   7. Yaxk'in strength, power, superiority, greatness

   8. Mol   lead, control, group, unite

   9. Chen   just, honest, fair, upright

 10. Yax   innocence, chastity, candor, ingenuousness

 11. Zac   fast, quick, prompt, agile

 12. Ceh   delicacy, softness, fineness, tenderness

 13. Maac   personality, aplomb, gift, class

 14. K'ank'in attribute, style, trait, nature

 15. Muan   expertise, skill, aptitude, memory

 16. Pax   knock, hit, move, deviate

 17. K'ayab joy, cheerfulness, solace, peace

 18. Cumhu clean, tidy up, wash, purify

 19. Uayeb   rate, value, appreciate, esteem (short interval of 5 days)

In figure 5.1(a), we see two pyramids, of which one is in the normal position and the other inverted (note the dualism inherent in the image). On the upright pyramid there are nine steps on the left and nine on the right. These steps symbolize the 18 months of the year, according to the Haab calendar. If you go to chapter 3, figure 3.4, in the upper part of this drawing one can see the twenty days of the month of the Haab. In the equation $18 \times 20 = 360$, we have the number that represents the days of the year, but may also represent years, intervals, degrees, and so forth, given that mathematics were understood in this manner in the Mayan culture. Here, according to the English archaeologist J. Eric S. Thompson (1898–1975), a cultural dilemma emerges: in the Mayan calendar of 360 days, the five days that correspond to the Gregorian and Julian calendars are missing, Thompson says. Later we will clarify his observational error, but for now, the reader is advised to disregard his suggestion that the Maya spent those five "missing" days staying in their houses and getting drunk, because they considered this to be a period of bad luck!

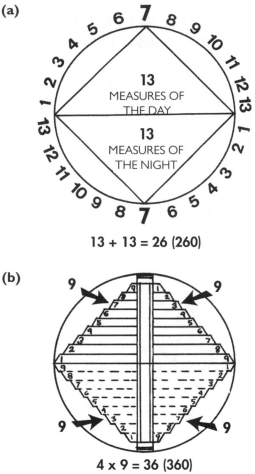

(a)

13
MEASURES OF
THE DAY

13
MEASURES OF
THE NIGHT

13 + 13 = 26 (260)

(b)

4 x 9 = 36 (360)

Figure 5.1 (a) Compare this drawing to figure 4.2 in chapter 4, which is from an image from the Chilam Balam and depicts thirteen marks that correspond to the division of the day into 13 intervals, or hours. Logically, if there are 13 hours in the day, there must correspondingly be 13 intervals, or hours, in the night. If we add day and night together, we have 26 intervals, or hours.

Figure 5.1 (b) depicts the Pyramid of Kukulcán, in the Yucatán. Note the two groups of nine steps in the upper part, one group on the right and one on the left, symbolizing the 18 months of the Haab, the solar calendar that the Maya used in common life to divide their year. Note that Mesoamerican culture perceived things dualistically, in pairs, and for this reason the number 18 is paired with another 18, yielding the number 36. If we append the *ge*, meaning "the principle," or the number 0, to this number, we obtain the number 360—another sacred number that the Maya used to measure days, intervals, degrees, and so forth.

The 20 Days of the Month
of the Haab Calendar

Here are the names of the 20 intervals, or days, of the Mayan Haab month, written correctly, in their proper order with their meanings. Fray Landa did not actually know how to write these names correctly in the language of the Itzae. Moreover, he never underwent the various initiatory degrees of the Mayan culture in which one learns about the sacred meanings attached to the various divisions of time. As an example, Landa wrote *K'ax yab,* when the correct spelling is *K'ayab,* meaning "joy, cheerfulness, solace, peace" or "many songs," to indicate that this month is close to springtime.

1.	Kan	vigor, sensibility, judgment, maturity
2.	Chicchan	knowledge, culture, erudition, wisdom
3.	Cimil	finish, change, remove, disappear
4.	Manik'	pass, continue, proceed, keep doing
5.	Lamat	penetrate, examine, deepen, analyze
6.	Muluc	near, around, adjacent, close
7.	Oc	traveler, walker, pilgrim, visitor
8.	Chuen	watch, observe, guard, heed
9.	Eb	rise, improvement, victory, mastery
10.	Ben	moderation, sanity, firmness, discretion
11.	Ix	rub, scratch, erode, rasp
12.	Men	creator, inventor, discoverer, innovator
13.	Cib	kind, tender, amiable, courteous
14.	Caban	beauty, harmony, equilibrium, peace
15.	Edznah	home, family, dwelling, temple
16.	Cauac	duality, couple, union, likeness
17.	Ahau	lord, master, initiate, guide
18.	Imix	origin, birth, beginning, foundation
19.	Ik'	transform, alter, vary, change
20.	Ak'bal	arcane, occult, mystical, esoteric

Mayan Numerology

Knowing the meaning behind the thirteen sacred numbers used by the Mayan people is essential to understanding the culture of our Mayan ancestors. Remember that this is only a brief explanation of the significance of each of the thirteen numbers. These numbers can also be read in *zuyua,* which means they can be read and understood backward, in reverse—but this more profound method of knowing will not be discussed or taught in this book.

0	Ge	The principle; the basis of the Mayan counting system; the cosmic egg; the spiral form of the ge symbolizes the source of our existence, the Milky Way.
I	Hun	Unity; beginning; the creative spark.
2	Ca	Knowledge of polarity and duality; a number of mystic vision as a result of the recognition of the conflict that comes with duality.
3	Ox	Activation and movement; growth stemming from intention (*x* is pronounced *sh* in Mayan).
4	Can	Definition and measurement; the four elements, the four directions, the four planes of existence; harmony and stability.
5	Ho	Empowerment and integration; the potential for choosing conflict or creativity that comes from being part of the whole; a number of inquiry, comparison, questioning.
6	Uac	Universal harmony and balance as we move through the cycles of change; intuitive flow; a number of equilibrium, development, and pursuit.

7	Uc	The number of chakras, of colors in the rainbow, of stars in the Pleiades; the number at the center of the number 13; the number of wisdom, focus, will.
8	Oaxac	Harmony, regeneration, restructuring, awareness of boundaries; a number of discovery, invention, and analysis.
9	Bolon	Number of completion; doorway to the next realm; the sum of the previous numbers and the number of supreme foundation.
10	Lahun	Intention and manifestation; completion of the will; a number of perfection of the physical; raw power into reality.
11	Hun lahun	As the energy of Hun and Lahun meet, chaos ensues, bringing release and healing of imbalance; the number of the healer who balances; only what serves the highest good carries through to the upper levels of energy.
12	Ca lahun	The crossroads; cycles preparing to end and the choices that come from such endings; a number of regeneration, rejuvenation, and the power of communication.
13	Ox lahun	Living with truth; perfection of the whole; prophecy and destiny; the beginning and the end; the clarity of the void.

As an example of Mayan numerology, let us consider the Mayan word for zero, *ge,* which means "the principle." The ancient Mayan civilization discovered and used the concept of zero before any other culture in the world (except for the Hindu culture of India, which used it strictly for astronomical calculations). *Ge* was depicted in the form of an eye because of its spiritual implications: it represents the Great Mystery, the essence of the beginning, the seed from which all of life springs forth. Physicists describe the zero point as a point of super-concentrated energy. According to Mayan philosophical thought, all existence has such a principle. When, for example, we append a 0 to the number 26, we obtain the number 260, which represents the sacred circle.

Now let us consider the number 9, *bolon,* meaning "final" or "limit." Note that when all the preceding numbers are added up, they ultimately add up to the number 9. The ancient Maya always used certain numbers to indicate things that were highly important in mathematics; wherever the number 9 appears, the end of some era is indicated. The mysterious 9 ought to be carefully studied in order to understand the Mayan culture. Here are some examples of how the number 9 is used in the Mayan context:

- A mixture of nine beverages was called Ixmucane, and this drink imparts strength and robustness; it creates muscles and makes the human being vigorous. According to the Popol Vuh, it was made by the progenitors Tepeu and Gugumatz.
- The number 9 is related to a calendar mentioned by the Spanish friar Diego de Landa, who recorded that the Maya performed their rites in March to celebrate the beginning of the year. This calendar is that of the equinoxes, the times when the sun crosses the equator, traveling from north to south or from south to north, in a trajectory lasting four-and-a-half Mayan months, until another extreme is reached. The same amount of time, four-and-a-half Mayan months, is required for the sun to return to the equator again, making a total of nine Mayan months.
- Ninety is the number of degrees between one cardinal point and the next. To draw a perfect square, 90-degree angles are needed; and the circle, as we have seen, contains four parts of 90 degrees each. The Haab has 4×90 intervals, but is adjusted every 52 years, and then it changes. At the beginning, however, it consists of 360 intervals, or days.

- Each season of the Mayan year lasts 91.25 days. The Pyramid of Kukulcán, in Chichén Itzá, in the Yucatán, has 91.25 steps. Likewise, the Mayan architects used 90-degree angles in constructing this pyramid.

- It takes Earth 9,360 Mayan hours, or intervals, to circle around the Sun; this is known as the Haab, or solar count; 130 intervals must be added to this measurement (corresponding to five days and nights, to adjust the calendar to 365), plus another 6.5 hours, or intervals, in a leap year, making a total adjusted time of 9,496.5 Mayan hours.

- Our solar system takes 9,490,000 intervals, or years, to make one complete revolution around the Pleiades and its center, Alcyone: this is the Great Calendar of the Suns, known as Tzek'eb in Mayan (recall that Tzek'eb is the Mayan name for the Pleiades), and it charts the 26,000-year cycle. Mayan oral tradition says that we are in the fifth sun of this great cycle.

- There are 9,461,500,000,000 kilometers in one light year, the distance traveled by light in the amount of time required by Earth to revolve once around the Sun (*Pequeño Larousse,* Barcelona: Editorial Noguer, 1972, p. 73). Contrast this with 9,496,500,000,000 Mayan kilometers—the distance traversed by a beam of light in the time taken by Earth to revolve once around the Sun. We should distinguish which of these two figures is correct: that of the Mayans or the preceding number given in the *Pequeño Larousse.*

The Mayan Clock

How did the Maya divide time in order that they might comprehend it better? For an explanation, we include an illustration of what is known as the Mayan clock. In figure 5.2 we see that one of our modern hours is equal to a Mayan hour of 50 minutes; the Mayan minute is 50 seconds; and one full cycle of day and night is 26 Mayan hours. Note

Figure 5.2. This illustration shows us how the Mayan numbers are used in the Mayan clock, which permits us to understand Mayan time better. What we have learned thus far in this regard will aid in the understanding of the investigations of the Mayan astronomical calendars that appear in this book.

that mathematically, the multiples of the Mayan clock yield the result 65,000; the first two numbers in this sum should be considered with particular care: the number 65, which is one quarter of 260, is the number of the Tzolk'in, the sacred Mayan calendar.

360 Mayan Degrees

Let us now consider figure 5.3. As you, dear reader, can see, this is yet another representation of the geometric and mathematical symbol of Hunab K'u, the Bearer of Movement and Measure, here depicted as the marker of degrees. People have been taught for a long time that

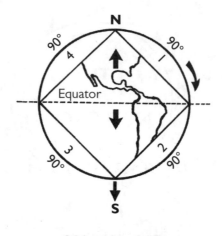

90° x 4 = 360°

Figure 5.3. Here again is the geometric form of Hunab K'u, the Bearer of Movement and Measure. The geometric form shows the number 90 four times, here indicating 90 degrees. The horizontal diameter marks the equator passing through the American continent. The upper and lower extremes indicate the North and South poles of the terrestrial globe.

the division of the circle into 360 degrees is the product of European culture; but upon seeing this drawing, it is clear that this division into 360 degrees was not only known to the Maya, but was used by them, many millennia before the Europeans began to use this in their mathematics.

6

THE SYNCHRONIZED
CALENDARS OF THE MAYA

Archaeologists and scholars have tended to see the Mayan calendar system through the prism of their own obscurations, regarding time the same way the European calendars marked it: with a focus on material, linear reality. For this reason they have been unable to answer the question of why Mesoamerican peoples spent so much time recording time.

The answer to this riddle is that our ancestors were not recording time; they were recording *timing*. The Mayan sages understood time as an endless web of cycles within cycles, all connected by an infinite spiral of the eternal Now. The Mayan calendars are thus reflections of exquisitely proportioned numerical systems, as well as a means of recording the harmonics that relate not only to space and time, but to the resonant qualities of Hunab K'u, of being and experience.

The Tzolk'in: The Master Calendar

Let us delve into the subject of the sacred Tzolk'in, also known as the calculation of destiny or the divinatory calendar, because it provides the patterns of the past, current, and future course of events. This calendar connects the energy of heaven with Earth so that what occurs above is reflected below; it has been in use by human beings for at least 3,000 years. The Tzolk'in is not based on the movements of our Sun, Earth, or any other planet in our solar system. It is synchronized with the movement of energy and consciousness in our galaxy—Hunab K'u—so that all the other cycles of stars, planets, and so forth follow from this Tzolk'in. The Mayan ancestors believed that by aligning themselves in this way, they could live in spiritual harmony with all of life and with nature.

The ancient Maya used more than seventeen different calendars—all of which were synchronized with the Tzolk'in, the master calendar that contains all the numerical patterns found in the other calendars. In fact, in the ancient Mayan world, the more calendars you knew, the greater your level of spiritual mastery. Though we will never truly know exactly how many calendars the Maya used because of Diego de Landa's destruction of the Mayan codices, it is certain that they were all synchronized with this sacred calendar, which is in itself a reflection of Hunab K'u.

According to my own investigations, the Tzolk'in serves as a mathematical synchronizer for understanding time and natural laws, including those that govern human beings. It is composed of the numbers 13 and 20, which, when multiplied, yield 260, a number that may represent days, intervals, degrees, and so forth. It is divided into four parts, thus forming a very important part of the Haab, the everyday calendar of the Maya, since both calendars cover the same period of time. Thus to understand the Haab correctly, the Tzolk'in must be available. The Tzolk'in was very important in Mayan rituals, since these had to take place at the mathematically correct times. For the Mayan priests of old, it was necessary to know and apply all the predictions of this calendar, not only for humans—a priest had to be able to baptize a new being, give it a name, and interpret its destiny according to what was indicated by the sacred Tzolk'in—but for nature and for the cosmos, too, so that human beings could harmonize with nature.

The Tzolk'in also tracks Mayan hours; for example, the 13 hours of day and the 13 hours of night, making a total of 26 hours. If these hours are multiplied by 10, the result is 260 Mayan hours. Remember also that the Mayan month has 20 days, which means that a Mayan month has 520 Mayan hours. Because our Mesoamerican culture regards all things in terms of pairs, or dualistically, 2 Mayan months make 40 days. These 40 days contain 1,040 hours, or intervals. This number of 1,040 has been used for years by mainstream scholars, but no scholar until now has made the conclusion I now arrive at: namely, that this number of 1,040 indicates hours, or intervals.

13 x 20 = 260

Figure 6.1. This illustration is from the Aztec Calendar, or the Stone of the Sun. The original calendar is in the National Museum of Anthropology in Mexico City. This calendar, made of stone, weighs 22 tons and measures 3.70 by 3.90 meters. As one can see from this illustration, there are 13 intervals in the upper square part and 20 intervals in the circle part. The carvings are the hieroglyphs of the Nahua people. If we multiply these two numbers, 13 x 20 = 260, the result is a new indicator for days, intervals, degrees, and so forth—thus demonstrating that both the Mayan and the Nahua peoples used the same sacred calendar.

The Tzolk'in appeared in the cultures of other Mesoamerican peoples, such as the Nahua, from the area around present-day Mexico City. Their name for this sacred calendar was Tonalamatl, which is known as the so-called Aztec Calendar (see figure 6.1) and can be seen today in the Museum of Anthropology and History in Mexico City. These Nahua people probably used this sacred calendar in a very similar manner in which we Maya used it. One can see on the Tonalamatl the 13 marks and 20 glyphs that symbolize the days of the Nahua month (13 × 20 = 260). These two sacred calendars, the Tzolk'in and the Tonalamatl, are in reality a single calendar, and as is well known among native peoples, they were highly important to all the Mesoamerican peoples. It is highly probable that other peoples, such as the Inca and Aymara, also used the same calendar, but with a different name, in accordance with their own languages.

The Haab

The Haab is based on the cycles of Earth and has 365 solar days, hence it was used by the Mayan people in common life and in agriculture. The Haab uses 18 months of 20 days each. Recall from chapter 2 our discussion of the Tree of Life and its importance to the Maya and all the indigenous peoples of Mesoamerica: the Wacah Chan, the galactic center, is linked to Earth and the underworld through the Tree of Life. The Haab is the root system of the Tree of Life, while the sacred Tzolk'in is the foliage of the tree, radiating and transmitting a continual harmonic universal frequency. Thus the Haab and the Tzolk'in cannot be used separately. The branches of the tree may be cut off and it will grow new ones, such as what happened during previous dark cycles. But if the roots of the tree are cut off, the Tree of Life dies. When we work with both cycles, the Haab and the Tzolk'in, we are connecting the spirit and the body, bridging the microcosm and the macrocosm, creating our reality.

We will now discuss the specifics of how the Haab and Tzolk'in calendars synchronize. Let us take a look at figure 6.3; the upper cir-

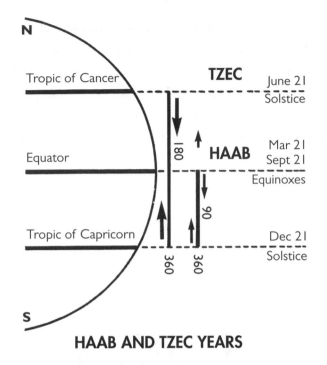

HAAB AND TZEC YEARS

Figure 6.2. The Maya tracked the solstices and the equinoxes through the Haab. The Spanish friar Diego de Landa wrote that when he was in the Yucatán, the Maya told him that their year began on a date that he tried to reconcile with the Gregorian calendar; they also told him they had other ways of measuring time, but unfortunately Fray Landa could not understand the first thing about how the Maya measured time.

cle is the Tzolk'in and the lower circle is the Haab. These two discs can revolve forward or backward; in this manner the years in the past or those in the future can be calculated accordingly. Note that the Tzolk'in, the smaller circle, has 13 and 20 divisions, and the Haab, the larger circle, has 18 and 20 divisions. If we perform a multiplication of the Tzolk'in, $13 \times 20 = 260$. A similar multiplication of the Haab, $18 \times 20 = 360$. If we add the number 5 (see page 86) to the 360 of the Haab, then add .25 (to account for the leap year in which one day is added every four years), we obtain 365.25. This quantity represents 365.25 days. In this manner we obtain a Mayan year that is the same as the year in the Gregorian and Julian calendars.

When archeologist J. Eric S. Thompson discussed the Haab in his theory of the Mayan calendars, he wrote that this calendar was lacking 5 days. But this assertion is not correct, because every 52 years the Maya adjusted their calendar to compensate for these 5 extra days. The Maya were accustomed to using their astronomical calendars for many years, and they adjusted them in cycles according to the numbers 13, 52, 104, 260, 520, 1040, etc. These numeric cycles may also have been used in microcosmic mathematical investigations as well as in macro-

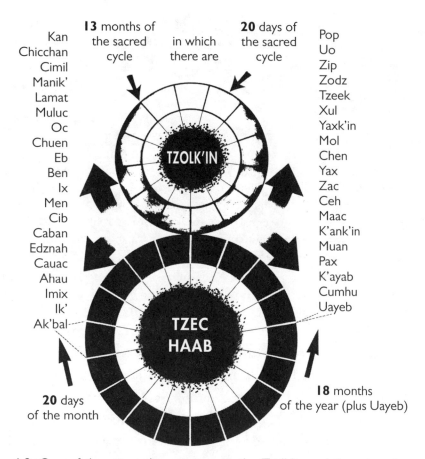

Figure 6.3. One of these two discs represents the Tzolk'in and the other the Haab; they revolve into both past and future. For example, 73 revolutions of the Tzolk'in equal 52 revolutions of the Tzec or Haab. This means that every 52 years, these two calendars were synchronized and in that very moment a new calendar of 52 years was formed. This calendar is known as Tunben K'ak'.

cosmic examinations of time. An example is the Mayan clock, figure 5.2 in the previous chapter, where the simplified result is the number 65, representing one quarter of the entire Tzolk'in.

Let us examine another example of how the Maya manipulated their astronomical calendars using the number 13, a key number in the Tzolk'in, as a synchronizer with the Haab. Over a period of 52 years, there are 13 leap days in the Haab. Every 52 years, the seven stars of the Pleiades would align in a certain place in the sky that the Maya had determined in advance. They would celebrate this event, calling it the New Fire. Thus this number 13 functions as a magical, cosmic number for working with the Mayan astronomical calendars.

The Tzolk'in calendar and the Haab or Tzec calendar get synchronized mathematically every 52 years. For example:

$$13 \text{ years} \times 4 \text{ cycles} = 52 \text{ years}$$
$$360 \text{ days} \times 13 \text{ years} = 4{,}680 \text{ days}; \ 4 \text{ cycles} \times 4{,}680 \text{ days} = 18{,}720 \text{ days}$$
$$(\text{or } 52 \text{ years})$$
$$\text{each year has 5 additional days} \times 52 = 260 \text{ days}$$
$$\text{there are 13 leap days in 52 years}$$
$$\text{Total} = 18{,}720 + 260 + 13 = 18{,}993 \text{ days, exactly 52 years}$$

The Tunben K'ak', or Pleiadian Cycle

Throughout Mesoamerica, native peoples had enduring memories of Pleiadians who came to Earth to teach and work with the four root races: the red, black, yellow, and white corn peoples in the introduction of this book. When they departed to return to their star home, they left four gifts for humanity: a sacred pouch, a metal crown that looked like flowers, a seed of light, and a seed of time—the Mayan calendars. These four great gifts unite the Mayan people and give them strength and inspiration.

Due to their very precise methods of astronomical observation, the Maya established the cycle of Tunben K'ak', the New Fire, which is celebrated every 52 years in accordance with one of the lesser cycles of the Pleiades. The Nahua people called this very same cycle the Xiohmilpilli, while in Spanish it is called Fuego Nuevo. This calendar of Earth marking the Pleiadian 52-year cycle relates to both the Tzolk'in and Haab. At the end of a Tunben K'ak' calendar cycle, the New Fire ceremony was performed. All the village fires would be extinguished during a ritual of fasting and prayers during the night. When the sun rose the next morning, gifts were made to the gods, and a new fire was lit by priests, who then carried it through the village to relight the hearths.

The archaeologist J. Eric S. Thompson used the figure 18,720 as the number of days used to synchronize the Tzolk'in and Haab calendars. However, Thompson did not understand what we will indicate in the following two points, showing the adjustment of the calendar cycles:

1. The number 260 represents the extra days that collect every 52 years. In this, one can see the masterful manner in which the Maya used mathematics: the number 260 corresponds to the Tzolk'in, the sacred calendar that synchronizes all the other calendars.
2. There are the 13 leap days that must be counted every 52 years for the calendar to be mathematically correct.

Thus every 52 Haabs and 73 Tzolk'ins (18,980 days), the original combination of day positions recurs, and the two counts return to their original starting position. The equation looks like this: $18{,}720 + 260 + 13 = 18{,}993$ days in one 52-year cycle of Tunben K'ak', combined with the Haab calendar of 52 years. This is the manner in which the Maya adjusted their astronomical calendars.

The following analysis further illustrates the aforementioned explanation of the 52-year cycle of the Maya with an aspect of duality, mentioned in the previous chapter.

52 years x 2 cycles = 104 years
18,720 days x 2 cycles = 37,440 days (or 104 years)
260 days x 2 cycles = 520 days
13 leap days x 2 cycles = 26 leap days
Total = 37,440 + 520 + 26 = 37,986 days, exactly 104 years

These numbers can be converted into mathematical keys for understanding the Mayan astronomical calendars:

1. In European thought, the circle in the square is represented by the number 100; for the Maya, the circle in the square—the geometry of Hunab K'u—is represented by the number 104, a number that is key to the Mayan social order of "As above, so below."

2. For the quantity 37,440 to give us exactly 104 years, we must add 520 more days, and another 26 leap days. The total is 37,440 + 520 + 26 = 37,986 days.

3. Observe that the number 520 is exactly twice the number of the Tzolk'in. This is the other key number for understanding the Mayan astronomical calendars.

4. Here we see the number 26 yet again, and we must return to the principle for understanding the mathematics and calendars of the Maya (see figure 4.2, in chapter 4). Note that in the illustration of the Mayan clock in the previous chapter, figure 5.2, the number 26 marks the hours; in number 4 of the chart above, it marks the leap days. In this manner, the number 26 is also a key number for understanding the Mayan astronomical calendars.

The Tun Uc

We now come to the Tun Uc, a lunar calendar that mirrors a woman's 28-day moon cycle. Mayan culture teaches us that women have a close relationship with the Moon and are in communion with it. Their lunar rites would begin at puberty and continue throughout life. In certain places, such as the Mayan temples of Uxmal, in the Yucatán, the Mayan women celebrated their monthly rituals by moonlight on particular nights in the lunar Tun Uc. Men were strictly prohibited from intruding on these rituals; this was because throughout Mesoamerica, women were closely associated with the Moon, whereas men were associated with the Sun—another example of dualism in Mesoamerican culture. Here again we note that the word *Uc* means the Moon; it is also interpreted as the number 7. The Maya believed in a close relationship between human beings (whether women or men), the number 7, and the Moon.

The Tun Uc is composed of 28-day months, with each month consisting of four cycles of 7 days each, and each year consisting of 13 months. This equates as: $28 \times 13 = 364$ days. This lunar calendar can be seen at the Pyramid of Kukulcán. As you can see in figure 3.4 from chapter 3, this pyramid has ninety-one steps. Multiplying the number 91 by 4 yields 364, which is the same total as in the preceding equation: $28 \times 13 = 364$.

Now we will cite an investigator who exhibits real knowledge concerning the laws of the Moon, and whose writings have a great deal to offer concerning our Mayan culture and the lunar calendar. Psychiatrist Arnold L. Lieber, in his book *El influjo de la luna* (published in English as *How the Moon Affects You,* and other titles on the same theme), discusses the importance of the Moon in society as well as in nature:

> The relevance of stress was explored by the biologist Harry Rounds, at Wichita State University, who took an interest in behaviors caused by the moon when, while investigating the blood factors of cockroaches, he discovered changes in their blood that were closely related to the phases of the moon. Intrigued, he decided to pursue the question further. He made comparisons of the blood of cock-

roaches, mice, and humans, and was able to detect chemicals that caused accelerated heartbeats. Aware that heartbeats are a categorical factor, the biologist divided his experimental subjects into two categories: those under stress and those not under stress. The acceleratory factors in the blood of the stressed animals increased a great deal shortly after the full and new moon. By contrast, cardioacceleratory factors were only found in the blood of non-stressed animals when the same factors reached a peak in the blood of the stressed animals; precisely after the blood activity of the stressed animals peaked, the blood activity of the non-stressed animals invariably descended to zero.

Why would the heartrates of cockroaches decrease after the full and new moon? Why would the hearts of humans and mice under stress beat more strongly during those periods? Mr. Round speculates that this is due to a change in the earth's electromagnetic field, brought about by the moon.

The Maya synchronized their Tun Uc with the Pyramid of Kukulcán every 52 years, according to a continuing system that included the Tzolk'in.

The Tzolk'in calendar and the Tun Uc or Lunar calendar get synchronized mathematically every 52 years. For example:

13 years x 4 cycles = 52 years
364 days x 52 years = 18,928 days (or 52 years)
1 additional day a year x 52 years = 52 days
there are 13 leap days in 52 years
Total = 18,928 + 52 + 13 = 18,993 days, exactly 52 years

We see that 18,928 days + 52 days + 13 leap days = 18,993 days in 52 years of the New Fire, which in Mayan is Tunben K'ak', combined with the lunar cycle of 52 years.

The K'altun

We now arrive at the Pleiadian calendar called the K'altun, or Wheel of the Katun. A katun is a count of 20 tuns (the word *tun* translates as "wheel"), which is 19.71 solar years, or something just short of 20 years in the European calendar. This calendar, which leads us through the great solar year of 26,000 years of the Pleiades, is comprised of 260 years and consists of 13 cycles of 20 years each, thus: 20 × 13 = 260 years, or one full K'altun. See figure 6.4, which depicts this Mayan calendar. According to the American archaeologist Sylvanus Morley (1883–1948), whose published work on the Mayan calendrical system has often been cited by Eurocentric scholars, the K'altun cycle is 19.77 years. But Morley was wrong. We shall see how the Maya truly understood this calendar in terms of mathematics.

Here, let us see how many days there are in the 260-year K'altun.

1. One year has   365 days
                         x 20 years of the K'altun
                         —————
                         7,300 days

2. Days of the K'altun: 7,300 days
                         x 13 cycles
                         —————
                         94,900 days, or 260 years of the K'altun

3. One K'altun has   5 leap days
                         x 13 cycles of 20 years
                         —————
                         There are 65 leap days in 260 years

4. One K'altun has   94,900 days
                         + 65 leap days
                         —————
                         94,965 days

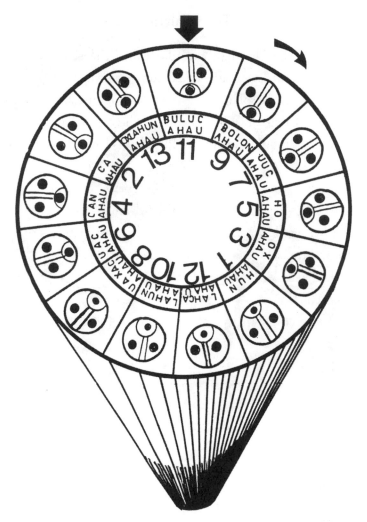

Figure 6.4. The Mayan K'altun, or Wheel of the Katun, consists of 13 cycles of 20 years each, making a total of 260 years, or 94,900 days plus 65 leap days, which yield a grand total of 94,965 days.

The K'altun cycle of 260 years is the key to understanding the great pattern behind the calendars, and here is why: The aspect of dualism in 260 years would be to add another 260 years, making 520 years. Each period of 520 years was known as the Tun K'aba (discussed in the next chapter). In fact, dear reader, this name for the 520-year period, Tun K'aba, has generally not been acknowledged by scholars of Mayan culture, the so-called Mayanists, since many of them have not comprehended the

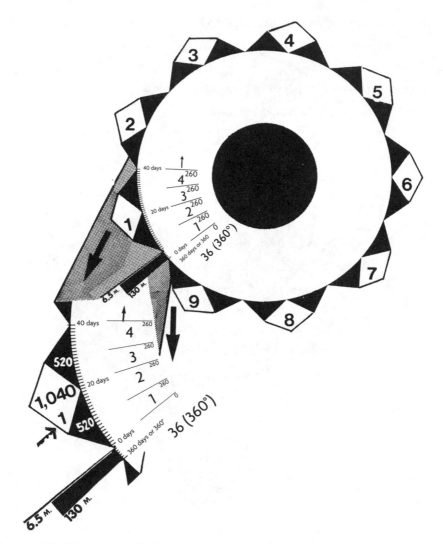

Figure 6.5. This is one of the most important illustrations in this book. As one can see, the disc with nine teeth represents a Mayan year, specifically the year of the Haab calendar. Each of the nine teeth on the outside of the disc is divided into two intervals; these intervals represent the 18 months of the Haab year.

In the part of the drawing that is separate from the disc, one can see the number 1,040 near the bottom, as well as the number 1, indicated by an arrow. This number 1 is one of the nine numbers of the toothed disc. By multiplying we arrive at the following equation: 9 × 1,040 = 9,360, which is the total Mayan hours in one year of the Haab. If 130 hours (see below: corresponding to five days and nights, to adjust the calendar to 365) are added, plus another 6.5 hours (see below: required to adjust to the Mayan fundamentals of Mayan calendrics. Once again applying the concept of dualism to the Tun K'aba, the cycle of 520 years, we arrive at a new sum: 1,040 years. Just as in Europe people count in millennia—1,000-year increments—so the Maya use 1,040 as their key number for counting the long term (see figure 6.5). And so the number 1,040, which is 4 × 260, is another key to understanding the Mayan Great Year (a 26,000-year cycle).

The Tzek'eb

To begin our consideration of the Tzek'eb, or Great Calendar of the Suns, which is a Pleiadian calendar with three methods of calculation, let us first examine some important statements found in the Popol Vuh:

> Immediately the surface of Earth dried due to the Sun. The Sun manifested himself, appearing like a man, and his face burned as he dried the surface of Earth. Before the Sun appeared, the surface of Earth was damp and muddy; but the Sun rose up and walked like a man [refer to chapter 4, figure 4.2]. But his heat could not be tolerated. He only manifested when he was born, and then became fixed like a mirror. He was certainly not the same Sun that we see, as is said in the legends of the Sun.

---

leap year), the resulting equation is: 9,360 + 130 + 6.5 = 9,496.5. This is the number of Mayan hours in one year of the Haab.

The following summarizes what we can understand from the numbers on this toothed disc, from the point of view of Mayan culture.

    26 hours in the day and night

  260 hours, corresponding to ten days and nights

  520 hours, corresponding to the twenty days in the Mayan month

1,040 hours, corresponding to two Mayan months

  130 hours, corresponding to five days and nights, to adjust the calendar to 365 days

   6.5 hours, required to adjust for the Mayan leap year

Let us linger for a moment on a couple of important statements here: *Before the Sun appeared, the surface of Earth was damp and muddy. . . . He was certainly not the same Sun that we see.* What this is telling us is that the Sun we see, our Sun, is a different sun: that is, the Maya knew of a sun that later changed into another sun—referring to the end of one solar cycle and the beginning of a new one. Undoubtedly this is a question of changes occurring on the cosmic level, which surely had an impact on Earth. And, certainly, these kinds of cosmic changes were recorded by the Maya in their renowned astronomical calendars, which could look backward and forward, since this was how the Mayan sages recorded all the astronomical phenomena that affected Mother Earth. For this reason, it is important to learn a little more about the Tzek'eb, the Great Calendar of the Suns.

After much investigation and contemplation, we realize that this calendar was used by the Maya to keep track of their suns, hence the name Tzek'eb. This calendar is related to the seven stars, or suns, of the Pleiades, which in the Mayan tradition are known as "the seven brothers of my father, the Sun." Recall that according to the Maya, life on Earth began when the Pleiades first reached the zenith. Accordingly, the Maya dedicated one of their calendars, the Tzek'eb, to the Pleiades.

We continued our investigation of the codices and pyramids, visiting many places in Mesoamerica, determined to find more proofs of the widespread existence of this particular calendar. We recalled the Stone of the Sun and the teachings of Maestro Esteban Serieys, mentioned in chapter 3, who says that this Nahua calendar was called the Tonal Machiotl, from *tonal,* "suns," and *machiotl,* "diagram," and means "diagram of the suns that have been and will be." There are four glyphs on the Stone of the Sun (see figure 6.1), representing the four ages through which Earth has lived, ages that were recorded in this stone by these native Mesoamericans who have so much to teach Europeanized culture. Thus our path was illuminated by this information from Maestro Serieys. With this knowledge, we were almost entirely sure that the Stone of the Sun is a cosmic indicator of the great cycles through which our solar system has passed—cycles that were indeed recorded by the Maya in their astronomical calendars.

Of course, we know that the ancient Mayan astronomers were well acquainted with the Pleiades; hence their name Tzek'eb, or Great Calendar of the Suns. This cosmic calendar, according to the Maya, encompassed 26,000 years and was used to keep track of the great solar cycles: specifically, the cycle of our solar system's orbit around the central star of the Pleiades, Alcyone, a giant star with a brilliance 1,400 times that of our Sun. The Mayan astronomical masters knew that our solar system is actually part of the system of the Pleiades, and that the Sun occupies the seventh orbit in this system—significantly, here again we find the number 7 in the relationship between our solar system and the Pleiades. Hence there were various reasons why the Maya called themselves Children of the Sun, and only one of them in reference to

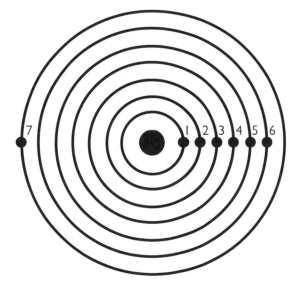

Alcyone (center)
1. Merope
2. Maia
3. Electra
4. Taygeta
5. Celaeno
6. Atlas
7. Our Solar System

Figure 6.6. The Pleiades, or Tzek'eb, constellation. Alcyone is the center of our stellar system: in other words, our solar system revolves around Alcyone every 26,000 years, as do a number of other suns, with their own orbital lengths. In this manner we are part of the Pleiades, or Tzek'eb. As can be seen from this illustration, our solar system occupies the seventh orbit around the Pleiades.

our own Sun. The Maya were one of the first peoples of the world to use this 26,000-year cycle of the Great Calendar of the Suns, which they did for the benefit of humanity. In our modern era, it is our obligation to take up this calendar once again, to educate and reeducate ourselves and the younger generations.

Let us refer to figure 6.5 for a moment: note the number 1,040, which refers to Mayan hours; this quantity is equivalent to two Mayan months. If one multiplies 1,040 hours by 9 (representing the dual Mayan months), the resulting equation is: $1,040 \times 9 = 9,360$ hours. If 130 more hours (corresponding to 5 days and nights that are absent from the 360-day year) are added to this number, and if an extra 6.5 hours are added to adjust for the Mayan leap year, then we arrive at the following equation: $9,360 + 130 + 6.5 = 9,496.5$ hours. This is the number of hours in one Mayan year.

Let us now see an example of how the Haab and the Tzek'eb synchronize: If we multiply 365 normal days by the 26,000 years in the Great Year of the Tzek'eb, we have the following equation: $26,000 \times 365 = 9,490,000$ days. But the leap days are missing from this quantity. Thus we must add 6,500 leap days, which correspond to 26,000 years. This yields $9,490,000 + 6,500 = 9,496,500$ days, which is the number of days in 26,000 years.

El pequeño Larousse defines a light year as "the distance a beam of light travels in one year, equivalent to 9,461,000,000,000 kilometers." This dictionary also says that every eighty years, the Gregorian or Julian calendar must be corrected, otherwise it will run late. Now let us consider the first quantity cited above, the 9,496,500 days used by the Maya to indicate 26,000 years, and we shall append six zeroes, resulting in 9,496,500,000,000, which we believe to be the correct number of kilometers in a light year, such a year being the amount of time, in kilometers, required by Earth to make one complete revolution around the sun.

The Mayan sages combined the Haab and Tzec calendars, using the Tzek'eb, along with the sacred Tzolk'in. In this manner, they brought many calendars together into a single one. Because the Mayan sages understood that all things that surround us are one, they conceived of everything as being structured in a mathematical cosmic unity. They understood their God as being the Single Giver of Movement and Measure, and gave him the name of Hunab K'u, the Sacred One. They also synchronized all their calendars, to measure cycles, distances, and dimensions. And they included the Sun, having declared him to be Father Sun.

But above all, kind reader, the Pleiadian calendars, which we shall discuss further in the next chapter, reveal that to the Maya, there is a dimension of the number 7 that rules us, whether we acknowledge it or not. And because this number 7 rules the forces of our bodies as well as the entire cosmos of which we are part, the Maya knew to integrate themselves into the cosmic laws that govern all things.

7

MATHEMATICAL METHODS FOR UNDERSTANDING THE CYCLES OF THE PLEIADES

Three different mathematical methods can be used to understand the cycles of the Pleiades and Tzek'eb, the Mayan Calendar of 26,000 years, discussed in the previous chapter.

According to information that I received directly from the Itzá Mayan tradition, the Tzek'eb calendar first began on March 21 of the year 3,373 BCE, when our Mayan ancestors saw the great sun Maia, of the Pleiades constellation, above the horizon of our Sun. It is worth noting once again that in the Mayan tradition, our Father Sun had seven brothers; together we all form a single cosmic family; the Maian solar system is one of the seven solar systems of the Pleiades.

For a better understanding of the numbers involved in the Tzek'eb, see the diagram that follows. The K'altun calendar, as we noted in chapter 6, leads us through the great solar year of the Pleiades, lasting 26,000 years; and in the Mayan calendars, the years have names as well as numbers. The Tzek'eb uses four names for each cycle of 520 years, which are derived from names of days from the Mayan Haab calendar. Every 520 years, these four names change and are replaced by four others taken from the Haab; this continues, with names changing every 520 years, until the point of 26,000 years is reached.

Below are the names of the years in the 520-year cycles, a quantity, we should note, that is the duality of the 260-year K'altun. The names in this chart begin at 3373 BCE and proceed through our current date and beyond, into the future, demonstrating 13 of the total 50 cycles of the Tzek'eb calendar.

THE TZEK'EB CALENDAR
3373 BCE, the beginning of the calendar

1.	Men (only in this cycle are there 260 years)		
	Chicchan		
	Ahau		Mayan year 260
	Oc	3373 − 260 = 3113 BCE	
2.	Cib		
	Cimil		
	Imix		260 + 520 = Mayan year 780
	Chuen	3113 − 520 = 2593 BCE	
3.	Caban		
	Manik'		
	Ik'		780 + 520 = Mayan year 1300
	Eb	2593 − 520 = 2073 BCE	
4.	Edznah		
	Lamat		
	Ak'bal		1300 + 520 = Mayan year 1820
	Ben	2073 − 520 = 1553 BCE	
5.	Cauac		
	Muluc		
	Kan		1820 + 520 = Mayan year 2340
	Ix	1553 − 520 = 1033 BCE	
6.	Ahau		
	Oc		
	Chicchan		2340 + 520 = Mayan year 2860
	Men	1033 − 520 = 513 BCE	

7. Imix
   Chuen
   Cimil   2860 + 520 = Mayan year 3380
   Cib   513 – 520 = 7 CE

8. Ik'
   Eb
   Manik'   3380 + 520 = Mayan year 3900
   Caban   7 + 520 = 527 CE

9. Ak'bal
   Ben
   Lamat   3900 + 520 = Mayan year 4420
   Edznah   527 + 520 = 1047 CE

10. Kan
    Ix
    Muluc   4420 + 520 = Mayan year 4940
    Cauac   1047 + 520 = 1567 CE

11. Chicchan
    Men
    Oc   4940 + 520 = Mayan year 5460
    Ahau   1567 + 520 = 2087 CE

12. Cimil
    Cib
    Chuen   5460 + 520 = Mayan year 5980
    Imix   2087 + 520 = 2607 CE

13. Manik'
    Caban
    Eb   5980 + 520 = Mayan year 6500
    Ik'   2607 + 520 = 3127 CE

Our current year, 2010, is indicated in cycle number 11. Our current cycle, like all the others, lasts 520 years; it began in the year 1567 and will end in the year 2087. The four names in our current cycle are:

Chicchan, Men, Oc, and Ahau. They must be used in this exact order, beginning with the first one and repeating this sequence of four in the same manner for all 520 years. After this, another four different names will be used, with this pattern continuing until another great solar cycle of the Pleiades has been completed—lasting, as we know, 26,000 years—the time required by our solar system and all its planets to make one complete revolution around Alcyone.

In cycle 13, the Mayan names used are: Manik', Caban, Eb, and Ik'. The 13th cycle marks one-quarter (6,500 years) of the 26,000-year Tzek'eb calendar.

The three methods for calculating the Tzek'eb calendar, two of which are explored in more detail below, are as follows:

$$6{,}500 \text{ years} \times 4 \text{ cycles} = 26{,}000 \text{ years}$$
$$2{,}600 \text{ years} \times 10 \text{ cycles} = 26{,}000 \text{ years}$$
$$1{,}040 \text{ years} \times 25 \text{ cycles} = 26{,}000 \text{ years}$$

2,600 years x 10 cycles = 26,000 years

This method also uses the twenty names of the Mayan days of the month; we begin by selecting the four names of Mayan months that will be used during a given 520-year period. For example, if we take the names *Chichan, Men, Oc,* and *Ahau,* which we will be using for our 520-year period, then multiply this quantity by 5, we get $520 \times 5 = 2{,}600$, which multiplied by 10 cycles gives us the 26,000 years of the Tzek'eb calendar. For a better understanding, here is a diagram in which one can see this mathematical method.

<u>20</u> days are in the Mayan month, and they have the following names: Kan, Chicchan, Cimil, Manik', Lamat, Muluc, Oc, Chuen, Eb, Ben, Ix, Men, Cib, Caban, Edznah, Cauac, Ahau, Imix, Ik', Ak'bal.

<u>4</u> names are selected to begin counting the cycle. For example (from cycle 11, in the previous chart). Chicchan, Men, Oc, Ahau.

5   is used as the multiplier for 4; remember that 5 x 4 = 20, the number of days in the Mayan Haab calendar.

520   years, composed of 130 Chicchan, 130 Men, 130 Oc, and 130 Ahau. The total number in this cycle is derived from: 4 x 130 = 520 years.

2,600   years resulting from the following multiplication: 5 x 520 = 2,600

26,000   years are in the Tzek'eb calendar, resulting from the multiplication of 10 x 2,600 = 26,000 years. Remember that this is the number of years our solar system takes to revolve once around the star Alcyone. As we know, Alcyone is the most important star in the Pleiades, and we ourselves are part of this constellation.

6,500 years x 4 cycles = 26,000 years

When we multiply the cycle of 6,500 years by 4, we get the following equation: 4 x 6,500 = 26,000; as we noted previously, this is the number of years our solar system takes to revolve once around the central star of the Pleiades, Alcyone. The ancient Maya must surely have used this 6,500-year system. Following are a series of observations taken from various sources that proves that the Maya used this number, 6,500, for tracking other celestial bodies.

The Great Sphinx, created by the armies of Egypt, was built in the Age of Leo; as is well known, its form resembles that of a lion. Of course, we are currently in the Age of Aquarius, and according to my calculations, 13,000 years have passed since the Age of Leo until now. According to the 26,000-year Tzek'eb calendar, this number, 13,000, marks the halfway point in the cycle of 26,000 years.

On September 13, 2005, the newspaper *Diario de Yucatán* published an article titled "Piramides en el Fondo Marino." This article says that between the Yucatán Peninsula and Cuba, there is an island submerged

700 meters beneath the sea. Also between the Yucatán and Cuba, but closer to the island of Cuba, Canadian and Cuban scientists have found enormous megalithic structures.

The Cuban geologist Manuel Iturralde Vinent has theorized that this island was the site of a complex of pyramids, built about 12,000 or 13,000 years ago. The Russian-Canadian geologist Paulina Zelitsky is of the same opinion. This submerged island is in international waters, nine kilometers from San Antonio, Cuba, and eighteen hours by boat from the Yucatán, Mexico.

Furthermore, the Chicxulub Crater (the translation of *Chicxulub* is "tail of the devil"), an ancient crater 180 kilometers in diameter, buried beneath the Yucatán Peninsula, was caused by an impact resembling an enormous atomic blast. The force liberated is said to be equivalent to fifty million nuclear bombs; such was the magnitude of the meteorite that smashed into Earth 65 million years ago. Of course, the number 65 appears repeatedly as one of the Mayan keys for understanding important things; the reader will recall that the number 65 is one quarter of 260, which is the number used for interpreting the Mayan Tzolk'in calendar, a number that appears again and again as a synchronizer of time. It has appeared in the following forms: 6.5, 65, 650, 6500, and even as the period of 65 million years.

Comets have always entered our solar system periodically; it is not known with certainty how many times this has occurred, nor how many times it will happen again in the future. Most readers will remember the visit of Comet Hale-Bopp in 1996–97; according to the astronomers Alan Hale and Thomas Bopp, who discovered this comet, 200 other comets were also visible in cosmic space. Here an important detail emerges: according to these astronomers, the orbital period of this comet is about 3,000 years, but I believe this figure ought to be adjusted to 3,250 years. My adjustment is supported by the following multiplication: $8 \times 3,250 = 26,000$ years. Thus it is possible that the ancient Maya used the Tzek'eb calendar for tracking Comet Hale-Bopp; according to Mayan timing, this comet would then have been observed every 3,250 years.

Pleiadian Eras: The Four Suns

Let us refer again to the Tonal Machiotl, or the Aztec Stone of the Sun (see figure 7.1). At the center of this calendar, one can see the history of all the suns, as well as the manner in which the indigenous peoples of Mesoamerica lived for many thousands of years. These ancient peoples knew that various different suns, or eons, had occurred, and they also knew when each sun ended, and that Earth underwent great changes whenever this kind of shift occurred. These shifts are related to the 26,000-year cycle of the Pleiades.

Among the many great changes that took place at the end of a sun, it is worth mentioning the disappearance of the race of giants that once inhabited Earth. When you go to visit the various pyramids of the Americas, you will find evidence that a race of gigantic beings built these monuments. At the Pyramid of K'inich K'ak'mu (or Kinich-Kakmó, as it is sometimes spelled), in Izamal, Yucatán, Mexico, the steps are not built for normal-size people, who might measure 1.7 meters (or 5 feet 7 inches) tall on average; rather, the steps are more suited for people 3 meters (or almost 10 feet) tall—the people who would have originally climbed this pyramid. This race of beings apparently disappeared when some great change occurred on the planet, brought about by a change in the sun—that is to say, when one sun ended and another sun began.

The second sun must have brought with it a great many hurricanes with very strong winds, just as we experience today in the Yucatán. Every year, several hurricanes come, with winds ranging from 50 to 400 kilometers per hour. These winds may even be stronger than the tornadoes that occur farther north in the United States. Thus we can be sure that in the past, humanity was also assaulted by strong winds as the second sun emerged. As we know, nature is capable of producing massive phenomena, such as the winds that occur when one sun gives way to the next.

The third sun brought with it great deluges that submerged many places on Earth. These great disasters were recorded by the Maya, as confirmed by the Dresden Codex. From this codex, we learn that the planets Venus, Mars, Mercury, and Jupiter played a part in this cataclysm. Surely some phenomenon must have occurred whereby the Sun affected these planets, resulting in floods on Earth; or else Earth trembled as a result of the cosmic changes, causing the oceans to overflow. In any case, the result was that humanity was virtually exterminated. As indicated by the Aztec Tonal Machiotl, this is another way one sun ended and another began.

Figure 7.1. This illustration shows the center of the Aztec Tonal Machiotl, or Stone of the Sun. This illustration is annotated with the numbers 1 through 4, indicating the four solar ages, or four suns, during which our Planet Earth has been inhabited by human beings. For the Maya, each sun has a cycle of 26,000 years. According to Mayan tradition, when the end of a solar cycle is reached, great changes occur on Earth, and very probably throughout our entire solar system. We are currently in the fifth sun, according to our cosmic Tzek'eb calendar, which tells us that four previous suns, or four 26,000-year solar cycles, have already passed. This means that 104,000 years have passed according to the Mayan cosmic calendar.

The beginning of the fourth sun almost exterminated humankind by fire, according to the Tonal Machiotl. In ancient times, the Maya lived in caves such as those of Loltún, Oxk'intok, Xtacumbilxunaan, and many others. This should not be confused with the Stone Age, during which time humans also lived in caves. If the Maya lived in caves, it was for no other reason than that it was difficult to survive on the surface of Earth. Indeed, it is possible that the Sun may have scorched a great part of Earth's surface, or else there were many volcanic eruptions on Earth, causing the surface of our planet to become overheated. Thus, finally, another era began, which was called the Solar Age of Fire by the Mesoamerican peoples.

These are the four eras, or suns, that are indicated in the central part of the Tonal Machiotl, or Stone of the Sun. Many authors ascribe a much shorter duration to the cycles of these eras; some give their duration as 676 years, some as 312 years, some even as short as 52 years. For my part, I consider the duration of these cycles to be 26,000 years, according to the manner in which I understand them. By this reckoning, it becomes apparent that each sun has been connected to the Pleiades, and especially to Alcyone; this is the manner in which our Pleiadian cosmic solar family, which includes our solar system, lives.

As discussed in chapter 1, the Itzá Maya claim that they originally came from Atlantis, or Atzantiha, during the time when the waters swallowed the font of wisdom. This probably occurred when one of the suns reached its end; most likely it was at the end of the last sun. At that time, the great changes that were brought about on Earth caused the waters to flood the continent of Atzantiha.

The Numerology of the Tzolk'in and the Lunar Tun Uc Calendar

The manner in which the sacred Mayan Tzolk'in calendar regulates the lunar Tun Uc calendar will now be demonstrated. The chart in figure

7.2, which uses the 13:20 matrix first revealed by Tony Shearer in his *Lord of the Dawn,* and amplified and described as the Loom of Maya by José Argüelles in *The Mayan Factor,* will serve as the basis for this exploration. As one can see, some letters run horizontally, and each of these letters has a dash after it; some letters are also arranged vertically. There are thirteen vertical columns and twenty horizontal rows, with a number inside each square.

To review, the Tzolk'in is formed by the numbers 13 and 20; multiplying them yields the equation $13 \times 20 = 260$. This, then, is the

	A-	B-	C-	D-	E-	F-	G-	H-	I-	J-	K-	L-	M-	
A	1	8	2	9	3	10	4	11	5	12	6	13	7	1
B	2	9	3	10	4	11	5	12	6	13	7	1	8	2
C	3	10	4	11	5	12	6	13	7	1	8	2	9	3
D	4	11	5	12	6	13	7	1	8	2	9	3	10	4
E	5	12	6	13	7	1	8	2	9	3	10	4	11	5
F	6	13	7	1	8	2	9	3	10	4	11	5	12	6
G	7	1	8	2	9	3	10	4	11	5	12	6	13	7
H	8	2	9	3	10	4	11	5	12	6	13	7	1	8
I	9	3	10	4	11	5	12	6	13	7	1	8	2	9
J	10	4	11	5	12	6	13	7	1	8	2	9	3	10
K	11	5	12	6	13	7	1	8	2	9	3	10	4	11
L	12	6	13	7	1	8	2	9	3	10	4	11	5	12
M	13	7	1	8	2	9	3	10	4	11	5	12	6	13
N	1	8	2	9	3	10	4	11	5	12	6	13	7	14
Ñ	2	9	3	10	4	11	5	12	6	13	7	1	8	15
O	3	10	4	11	5	12	6	13	7	1	8	2	9	16
P	4	11	5	12	6	13	7	1	8	2	9	3	10	17
Q	5	12	6	13	7	1	8	2	9	3	10	4	11	18
R	6	13	7	1	8	2	9	3	10	4	11	5	12	19
S	7	1	8	2	9	3	10	4	11	5	12	6	13	20
	1	2	3	4	5	6	7	8	9	10	11	12	13	

Figure 7.2

numerology of the Tzolk'in, represented in figure 7.2. So we can see that this diagram has 260 squares, with a number inside each square. To understand this diagram of the Tzolk'in, one must begin with the number 1 and continue progressively until one arrives at 13. Then one must begin anew with the number 1, until one reaches 7; if these are added, the result is 13 + 7 = 20. In this way, one can begin to see how the Tzolk'in explains the functioning of lunar energy by means of mathematics.

The following four examples show how to locate the number 28 in the lunar cycle, that is, by following the letters indicated. The lines drawn on figures 7.3, 7.4, and 7.5 show the different ways to get the number 14, which added to the opposite squares, gives us the total of 28. Whenever the drawing is traversed in order to determine the numeric combinations, one must always pass through the central point in the diagram, between the numbers 13 and 1. Four squares are added together each time. The lines move as if they were hands on a clock but moving in opposite directions.

A, A − (1) + S, M − (13) = 14   A, B − (8) + S, L − (6) = 14

A, M − (7) + S, A − (7) = 14   A, L − (13) + S, B − (1) = 14
$$\overline{\quad 28 \quad}$$ $$\overline{\quad 28 \quad}$$

A, C − (2) + S, K − (12) = 14   A, D − (9) + S, J − (5) = 14

A, K − (6) + S, C − (8) = 14   A, J − (12) + S, D − (2) = 14
$$\overline{\quad 28 \quad}$$ $$\overline{\quad 28 \quad}$$

As one can see from these four examples, the mathematical sum is always 28, namely, the number of days in the lunar cycle. In this masterful way, the Mayan sages created their lunar calendar, which can be explained by means of the Tzolk'in. Figures 7.3, 7.4, and 7.5 show

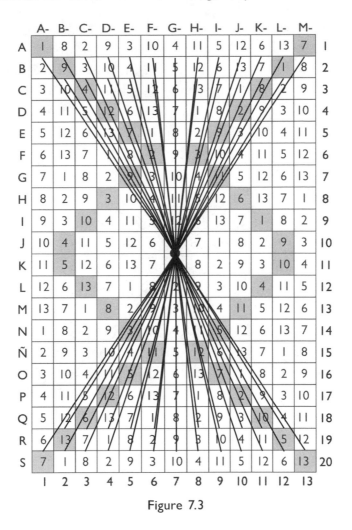

Figure 7.3

some of the other mathematical combinations one can make in order to understand the great manifestation of lunar energy. By my understanding, a prodigious number of different lunar energy frequencies are revealed here.

I am certain, dear reader, that the sacred, divinatory, magical Tzolk'in was used by the Maya for understanding the functioning of the energy of the planets in our solar system. This sacred calendar was expressed mathematically, enabling the Mayan sages to decipher the cycles and movements of the planets. In such a fashion, the Tzolk'in was the codifier of the planets.

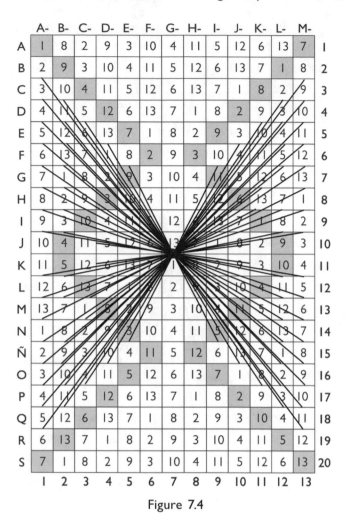

Figure 7.4

This sacred calendar was also mathematically synchronized with various other calendars, with the Pleiades, and with the various suns in the Pleiades, the center of which is the great star Alcyone, around which our solar system orbits in a cycle of 26,000 years.

Only Hunab K'u knows how much the Maya truly knew. The investigations we have presented in this book were inspired by the Tzolk'in, and with them we have penetrated the wisdom of the eternal Mayan God. Our Mayan God, who is wisdom and intelligence, is the architect of the universe and creator of all that exists. Hunab K'u created human beings and gave them all their potentialities; he also gave them

	A-	B-	C-	D-	E-	F-	G-	H-	I-	J-	K-	L-	M-	
A	1	8	2	9	3	10	4	11	5	12	6	13	7	1
B	2	9	3	10	4	11	5	12	6	13	7	1	8	2
C	3	10	4	11	5	12	6	13	7	1	8	2	9	3
D	4	11	5	12	6	13	7	1	8	2	9	3	10	4
E	5	12	6	13	7	1	8	2	9	3	10	4	11	5
F	6	13	7	1	8	2	9	3	10	4	11	5	12	6
G	7	1	8	2	9	3	10	4	11	5	12	6	13	7
H	8	2	9	3	10	4	11	5	12	6	13	7	1	8
I	9	3	10	4	11	5	12	6	13	7	1	8	2	9
J	10	4	11	5	12	6	7	1	8	2	9	3		10
K	11	5	12	6	13				2	9	3	10	4	11
L	12	6	13	7	8	2	9	3	10	4	11	5		12
M	13	7	1	8	2	9	3	10	4	11	5	12	6	13
N	1	8	2	9	3	10	4	1	5	12	6	13	7	14
Ñ	2	9	3	10	4	11	5	12	6	13	7	1	8	15
O	3	10	4	11	5	12	6	13	7	1	8	2	9	16
P	4	11	5	12	6	13	7	1	8	2	9	3	10	17
Q	5	12	6	13	7	1	8	2	9	3	10	4	11	18
R	6	13	7	1	8	2	9	3	10	4	11	5	12	19
S	7	1	8	2	9	3	10	4	11	5	12	6	13	20
	1	2	3	4	5	6	7	8	9	10	11	12	13	

Figure 7.5

the Tzolk'in, that they might use it to discover all the mysteries of life by means of mathematics.

I hope that this book of the Mayan astronomical calendars, with all that is taught in it, will serve as the basis for future investigations into the ways in which the Maya operated with cyclical time. At the same time, it is hoped that researchers will begin to truly understand the Tzolk'in, and that its energy will be treated with respect and used for the benefit of all living beings. This is a sacred teaching, which Hunab K'u imparted to the Maya and to all of humanity.

The Maya Are Here

Many people have asked: Where did the Maya go? I answer: The Mayan initiates are not gone; they are with us. One need only know how to perceive the dimension in which they exist: the Maya are illusion; they are the Children of the Sun; they are the children of time; they are thought itself. The Maya, if one contemplates, are illusion and the thought of time. In the present time, we must meditate in order to know whether we ourselves are also part of the illusion of time in its thought.

Once we have understood the great symbolism of these words, we will be prepared to listen to the Mayan masters; they will call to us. These Maya exist in a different dimensional level, from which they observe us, and yet we, with our blunted senses, deranged by this materialistic society, are unable to perceive them. For this reason, because of this delusion, we are not able to ascend to the state of purity that is necessary for perceiving that dimension in which the Mayan initiates exist. If we purify ourselves through meditations on the pyramids, we will be able to reach out to Hunab K'u, and he, with his wise cosmic intelligence, will show us the path traveled by the people who have paid homage to him through so many cycles. Let us therefore meditate with Father Sun in order to purify ourselves, and when we are ready, we will understand what these Mayan sages and initiates expect of us, in order that together we may find the alternative to this Europeanized society. And once we have all achieved this cosmic harmony, we will then be like the Maya: illusion and memory of time; and all together, we will shine like light in that other place, that other dimension.

BIBLIOGRAPHY

Argüelles, José. *Earth Ascending.* 2nd ed. Rochester, Vt.: Bear & Company, 1988.

———. *The Mayan Factor.* Rochester, Vt.: Bear & Company, 1996.

———. *Time and the Technosphere.* Rochester, Vt.: Bear & Comany, 2002.

Arochi, Luis E. *La Pirámide de Kukulcán y su símbolo solar.* Mexico City: Editorial Orión, S.A., 1977.

Benavides, Rodolfo. *Dramáticas profecías de la Gran Pirámide.* Mexico City: Editores Mexicanos Unidos, S.A., 1977.

Campo, Issa del. *Nuestra raza frente a sus ancestros.* Mexico City: Editorial Orión, 1965.

Churchward, Col. James. *The Children of Mu.* Albuquerque, N. Mex.: Brotherhood of Life, 1988.

———. *The Lost Continent of Mu.* Albuquerque, N. Mex.: Brotherhood of Life, 1987.

Darquea, Javier Cabrera. *El mensaje de las piedras Grabadas de Ica.* Peru: Inti Sol Editores y Distribuidores, S.A., 1980.

Duarte, Ignacio Magaloni. *Educadores del mundo.* Mexico City: Editor Costa Amic, 1969.

Ferrero, Luis. *Costa Rica Precolombina.* Costa Rica: Editorial Costa Rica, 1981.

Guirao, Pedro. *Mu, ¿paraíso perdido?* Spain: Producciones Editoriales, 1976.

Harleston, Hugh, Jr. *El misterio de las pirámides Mexicanas.* Mexico City: Editoriales de Mexico, S.A., 1978.

Ibarra Grasso, Dick Edgar. *Ciencia en Tiwanak'u y el Incaico.* Bolivia: Editorial Los Amigos del Libro, 1982.

Illeseas Cook, Guillermo. *Astrónomos en el antiguo Perú*. Peru: Kósmos Editores y Distribuidores, S.A., 1976.

Ivanoff, Pierre. *En el país de los Mayas*. Barcelona: Editorial Gráfica Guada, S.A., 1974.

Lieber, Arnold L. *El influjo de la luna*. Madrid: EDAF Editores Distribuidores, S.A., 1979.

Marin, Juan. *El Egipto de los faraones*. Santiago de Chile: Zig-Zag, 1955.

Martinez Paredez, Domingo. *Hunab K'u, Síntesis del pensamiento filosófico Maya*. Mexico City: Editora Cusamil, S.A., 1973.

Mediz Bolio, Antonio. *The Books of the Chilam Balam of Chumayel*. Suzanne D. Fisher, trans. Available at: http://myweb.cableone.net/subru/Chilam .html#anchor3390178myweb.cableone.net

Men, Hunbatz. *Secrets of Mayan Science/Religion*. Rochester, Vt.: Bear & Company, 1990.

Shearer, Tony. *Lord of the Dawn*. 2nd ed. Happy Camp, Calif.: Naturegraph Publishers, 1995.

INDEX

Page numbers in *italics* represent figures.

Books of Related Interest

Secrets of Mayan Science/Religion
by Hunbatz Men

Maya Cosmogenesis 2012
The True Meaning of the Maya Calendar End-Date
by John Major Jenkins

Galactic Alignment
The Transformation of Consciousness According to Mayan,
Egyptian, and Vedic Traditions
by John Major Jenkins

How to Practice Mayan Astrology
The Tzolkin Calendar and Your Life Path
by Bruce Scofield and Barry C. Orr

The Mayan Calendar and the Transformation of Consciousness
by Carl Johan Calleman, Ph.D.

The Purposeful Universe
How Quantum Theory and Mayan Cosmology Explain the
Origin and Evolution of Life
by Carl Johan Calleman, Ph.D.

The Mayan Code
Time Acceleration and Awakening the World Mind
by Barbara Hand Clow

Return of the Children of Light
Incan and Mayan Prophecies for a New World
by Judith Bluestone Polich

INNER TRADITIONS • BEAR & COMPANY
P.O. Box 388
Rochester, VT 05767
1-800-246-8648
www.InnerTraditions.com

Or contact your local bookseller